AWS Command Line Interface User Guide

A catalogue record for this book is available from the Hong Kong Public Libraries.

Published in Hong Kong by Samurai Media Limited.

Email: info@samuraimedia.org

ISBN 9789888408061

Contents

What Is the AWS Command Line Interface?

The AWS CLI is an open source tool built on top of the AWS SDK for Python (Boto) that provides commands for interacting with AWS services. With minimal configuration, you can start using all of the functionality provided by the AWS Management Console from your favorite terminal program.

- **Linux shells** – Use common shell programs such as `Bash`, `Zsh`, and `tsch` to run commands in Linux, macOS, or Unix.

- **Windows command line** – On Microsoft Windows, run commands in either PowerShell or the Windows Command Processor.

- **Remotely** – Run commands on Amazon EC2 instances through a remote terminal such as PuTTY or SSH, or with Amazon EC2 systems manager.

The AWS CLI provides direct access to AWS services' public APIs. Explore a service's capabilities with the AWS CLI, and develop shell scripts to manage your resources. Or take what you've learned to develop programs in other languages with the AWS SDK.

In addition to the low level, API equivalent commands, the AWS CLI also provides customizations for several services. Customizations are higher level commands that simplify using a service with a complex API. For example, the `aws s3` set of commands provide a familiar syntax for managing files in Amazon S3.

Example Upload a file to Amazon S3

`aws s3 cp` provides a shell-like copy command, and automatically performs a multipart upload to transfer large files quickly and resiliently.

```
1 ~$ aws s3 cp myvideo.mp4 s3://mybucket/
```

Performing the same task with the low level commands (available under `aws s3api`) would take a lot more effort.

Depending on your use case, you may want to use the AWS SDK, a toolkit, or the AWS Tools for Windows PowerShell.

- AWS Tools for Windows PowerShell
- AWS SDK for Java
- AWS SDK for .NET
- AWS SDK for JavaScript
- AWS SDK for Ruby
- AWS SDK for Python (Boto)
- AWS SDK for PHP
- AWS SDK for Go
- AWS Toolkit for Eclipse
- AWS Toolkit for Visual Studio
- AWS Mobile SDK for iOS
- AWS Mobile SDK for Android

You can view—and fork—the source code for the AWS CLI on GitHub in the aws-cli repository. Join the community of users on GitHub to provide feedback, request features, and submit your own contributions!

Using the Examples in this Guide

The examples in this guide are formatted with the following conventions:

- **Prompt** – The command prompt is displayed as a dollar sign ('$'). Do not include the prompt when you type commands.

- **Directory** – When commands must be executed from a specific directory, the directory name is shown before the prompt symbol.

- **User Input** – Command text that you should enter at the command line is formatted as **user input**.

- **Replaceable Text** – Variable text, including names of resources that you choose, or IDs generated by AWS services that you must include in commands, is formatted as *replaceable text*. In multiple line commands or commands where specific keyboard input is required, keyboard commands can also be shown as replaceable text.

- **Output** – Output returned by AWS services is shown beneath user input without any special formatting.

For example, the following command includes user input, replaceable text, and output:

```
1 $ aws configure
2 AWS Access Key ID [None]: AKIAIOSFODNN7EXAMPLE
3 AWS Secret Access Key [None]: wJalrXUtnFEMI/K7MDENG/bPxRfiCYEXAMPLEKEY
4 Default region name [None]: us-west-2
5 Default output format [None]: ENTER
```

To use this example, type **aws configure** at the command line and press Enter. **aws configure** is the command. This command is interactive, so the AWS CLI outputs lines of texts, prompting you to enter additional information. Enter each of your access keys in turn and press Enter. Then, enter a region name in the format shown, press Enter, and press Enter a final time to skip the output format setting. The final Enter command is shown as replaceable text because there is no user input for that line. Otherwise, it would be implied.

The following example shows a simple non-interactive command with output from the service in JSON format:

```
1 $ aws ec2 create-security-group --group-name my-sg --description "My security group"
2 {
3     "GroupId": "sg-903004f8"
4 }
```

To use this example, enter the full text of the command (the highlighted text after the prompt) and press Enter. The name of the security group, my-sg is replaceable. In this case, you can use the group name as shown, but you will probably want to use a more descriptive name.

Note

Arguments that must be replaced (such as AWS Access Key ID), and those that should be replaced (such as group name), are both shown as *replaceable text*. If an argument must be replaced, it will be noted in the text describing the example.

The JSON document, including the curly braces, is output. If you configure your CLI to output in text or table format, the output will be formatted differently. JSON is the default output format.

About Amazon Web Services

Amazon Web Services (AWS) is a collection of digital infrastructure services that developers can leverage when developing their applications. The services include computing, storage, database, and application synchronization (messaging and queuing). AWS uses a pay-as-you-go service model. You are charged only for the services that you—or your applications—use. Also, to make AWS more approachable as a platform for prototyping and experimentation, AWS offers a free usage tier. On this tier, services are free below a certain level of usage. For more information about AWS costs and the Free Tier, see Test-Driving AWS in the Free Usage Tier. To obtain an AWS account, open the AWS home page and then click **Sign Up**.

Installing the AWS Command Line Interface

The primary distribution method for the AWS CLI on Linux, Windows, and macOS is `pip`, a package manager for Python that provides an easy way to install, upgrade, and remove Python packages and their dependencies.

Current AWS CLI Version
The AWS CLI is updated frequently with support for new services and commands. To see if you have the latest version, see the releases page on GitHub.

Requirements

- Python 2 version 2.6.5+ or Python 3 version 3.3+

- Windows, Linux, macOS, or Unix

Note
Older versions of Python may not work with all AWS services. If you see `InsecurePlatformWarning` or deprecation notices when you install or use the AWS CLI, update to a recent version.

If you already have `pip` and a supported version of Python, you can install the AWS CLI with the following command:

```
1 $ pip install awscli --upgrade --user
```

The `--upgrade` option tells `pip` to upgrade any requirements that are already installed. The `--user` option tells `pip` to install the program to a subdirectory of your user directory to avoid modifying libraries used by your operating system.

If you encounter issues when you attempt to install the AWS CLI with `pip`, you can install the AWS CLI in a virtual environment to isolate the tool and its dependencies, or use a different version of Python than you normally do.

Standalone Installers
For offline or automated installations on Linux, macOS, or Unix, try the bundled installer. The bundled installer includes the AWS CLI, its dependencies, and a shell script that performs the installation for you.
On Windows, you can also use the MSI installer. Both of these methods simplify the initial installation, with the tradeoff of being more difficult to upgrade when a new version of the AWS CLI is released.

After you install the AWS CLI, you may need to add the path to the executable file to your PATH variable. For platform specific instructions, see the following topics:

- **Linux** –

- **Windows** –

- **macOS** –

Verify that the AWS CLI installed correctly by running `aws --version`.

```
1 $ aws --version
2 aws-cli/1.11.84 Python/3.6.2 Linux/4.4.0-59-generic botocore/1.5.47
```

The AWS CLI is updated regularly to add support for new services and commands. To update to the latest version of the AWS CLI, run the installation command again.

```
1 $ pip install awscli --upgrade --user
```

If you need to uninstall the AWS CLI, use `pip uninstall`.

```
1 $ pip uninstall awscli
```

If you don't have Python and `pip`, use the procedure for your operating system:

- Install the AWS Command Line Interface on Linux
- Install the AWS Command Line Interface on Microsoft Windows
- Install the AWS Command Line Interface on macOS
- Install the AWS Command Line Interface in a Virtual Environment
- Install the AWS CLI Using the Bundled Installer (Linux, macOS, or Unix)

Install the AWS Command Line Interface on Linux

You can install the AWS Command Line Interface and its dependencies on most Linux distributions with `pip`, a package manager for Python.

Important
The `awscli` package is available in repositories for other package managers such as APT and yum, but it is not guaranteed to be the latest version unless you get it from `pip` or use the bundled installer

If you already have pip, follow the instructions in the main installation topic. Run `pip --version` to see if your version of Linux already includes Python and pip.

```
1 $ pip --version
```

If you don't have pip, check to see which version of Python is installed.

```
1 $ python --version
```

or

```
1 $ python3 --version
```

If you don't have Python 2 version 2.6.5+ or Python 3 version 3.3+, install Python. Otherwise, install pip and the AWS CLI.

- Installing Python on Linux
- Installing the AWS Command Line Interface on Amazon Linux 2017
- Installing Pip
- Installing the AWS CLI with Pip
- Adding the AWS CLI Executable to your Command Line Path

Installing Pip

If you don't have `pip`, install `pip` with the script provided by the Python Packaging Authority.

To install pip

1. Download the installation script from pypa.io:

```
1 $ curl -O https://bootstrap.pypa.io/get-pip.py
```

   The script downloads and installs the latest version of `pip` and another required package named `setuptools`.

2. Run the script with Python:

```
1 $ python get-pip.py --user
```

3. Add the executable path to your PATH variable: `~/.local/bin`

To modify your PATH variable (Linux, macOS, or Unix)

1. Find your shell's profile script in your user folder. If you are not sure which shell you have, run `echo $SHELL`.

```
1 $ ls -a ~
2 .  ..  .bash_logout  .bash_profile  .bashrc  Desktop  Documents  Downloads
```

   - **Bash** – `.bash_profile`, `.profile`, or `.bash_login`.
   - **Zsh** – `.zshrc`
   - **Tcsh** – `.tcshrc`, `.cshrc` or `.login`.

2. Add an export command to your profile script.

```
1 export PATH=~/.local/bin:$PATH
```

This command adds a path, `~/.local/bin` in this example, to the current PATH variable.

3. Load the profile into your current session.

```
1 $ source ~/.bash_profile
```

4. Verify that pip is installed correctly.

```
1 $ pip --version
2 pip 8.1.2 from ~/.local/lib/python3.4/site-packages (python 3.4)
```

Installing the AWS CLI with Pip

Use `pip` to install the AWS CLI.

```
1 $ pip install awscli --upgrade --user
```

Verify that the AWS CLI installed correctly.

```
1 $ aws --version
2 aws-cli/1.11.84 Python/3.6.2 Linux/4.4.0-59-generic botocore/1.5.47
```

If you get an error, see .

To upgrade to the latest version, run the installation command again:

```
1 $ pip install awscli --upgrade --user
```

Adding the AWS CLI Executable to your Command Line Path

After installing with `pip`, you may need to add the `aws` executable to your OS's PATH environment variable.

Example AWS CLI install location - Linux with pip (user mode)

```
1 ~/.local/bin
```

If you didn't install in user mode, the executable might be in the `bin` folder of your Python installation. If you don't know where Python is installed, run `which python`.

```
1 $ which python
2 /usr/local/bin/python
```

The output may be the path to a symlink, not the actual executable. Run `ls -al` to see where it points.

```
1 $ ls -al /usr/local/bin/python
2 ~/.local/Python/3.6/bin/python3.6
```

To modify your PATH variable (Linux, macOS, or Unix)

1. Find your shell's profile script in your user folder. If you are not sure which shell you have, run `echo $SHELL`.

```
1 $ ls -a ~
2 .  ..  .bash_logout  .bash_profile  .bashrc  Desktop  Documents  Downloads
```

- **Bash** – .bash_profile, .profile, or .bash_login.

- **Zsh** – `.zshrc`
- **Tcsh** – `.tcshrc`, `.cshrc` or `.login`.

2. Add an export command to your profile script.

```
1  export PATH=~/.local/bin:$PATH
```

This command adds a path, `~/.local/bin` in this example, to the current PATH variable.

3. Load the profile into your current session.

```
1  $ source ~/.bash_profile
```

Installing Python on Linux

If your distribution did not come with Python, or came with an older version, install Python before installing pip and the AWS CLI.

To install Python 3 on Linux

1. Check to see if Python is already installed:

```
1 $ python --version
```

Note

If your Linux distribution came with Python, you may need to install the Python developer package in order to get the headers and libraries required to compile extensions and install the AWS CLI. Install the developer package (typically named python-dev or python-devel) using your package manager.

1. If Python 2.7 or later is not installed, install Python with your distribution's package manager. The command and package name varies:

   - On Debian derivatives such as Ubuntu, use APT:

   ```
   1 $ sudo apt-get install python3
   ```

   - On Red Hat and derivatives, use yum:

   ```
   1 $ sudo yum install python
   ```

   - On SUSE and derivatives, use zypper:

   ```
   1 $ sudo zypper install python3
   ```

2. Open a command prompt or shell and run the following command to verify that Python installed correctly:

```
1 $ python3 --version
2 Python 3.6.2
```

Installing the AWS Command Line Interface on Amazon Linux 2017

The AWS CLI comes pre-installed on the Amazon Linux AMI. Check the currently installed version with `aws --version`.

```
1 $ aws --version
2 aws-cli/1.11.83 Python/2.7.12 Linux/4.9.20-11.31.amzn1.x86_64 botocore/1.5.46
```

You can use `sudo yum update` to get the latest version available in the yum repository, but this may not be the latest version. Use pip to get the latest version.

To upgrade the AWS CLI on Amazon Linux (root)

1. Use `pip install` to install the latest version of the AWS CLI.

```
1 $ sudo pip install --upgrade awscli
```

2. Verify the new version with `aws --version`.

```
1 $ aws --version
2 aws-cli/1.11.85 Python/2.7.12 Linux/4.9.20-11.31.amzn1.x86_64 botocore/1.5.48
```

If you don't have root privileges, install the AWS CLI in user mode.

To upgrade the AWS CLI on Amazon Linux (user)

1. Use `pip install` to install the latest version of the AWS CLI.

```
1 $ sudo pip install --upgrade --user awscli
```

2. Add the install location to the beginning of your `PATH` variable.

```
1 $ export PATH=/home/ec2-user/.local/bin:$PATH
```

Add this command to the end of `~/.bashrc` to maintain the change between sessions.

3. Verify the new version with `aws --version`.

```
1 $ aws --version
2 aws-cli/1.11.85 Python/2.7.12 Linux/4.9.20-11.31.amzn1.x86_64 botocore/1.5.48
```

Install the AWS Command Line Interface on Microsoft Windows

You can install the AWS CLI on Windows with a standalone installer or `pip`, a package manager for Python. If you already have `pip`, follow the instructions in the main installation topic.

- MSI Installer
- Install Python, pip, and the AWS CLI on Windows
- Adding the AWS CLI Executable to your Command Line Path

MSI Installer

The AWS CLI is supported on Microsoft Windows XP or later. For Windows users, the MSI installation package offers a familiar and convenient way to install the AWS CLI without installing any other prerequisites.

When updates are released, you must repeat the installation process to get the latest version of the AWS CLI. If you prefer to update frequently, consider using pip for easier updates.

To install the AWS CLI using the MSI installer

1. Download the appropriate MSI installer.

   - Download the AWS CLI MSI installer for Windows (64-bit)

   - Download the AWS CLI MSI installer for Windows (32-bit) **Note**
     The MSI installer for the AWS CLI does not work with Windows Server 2008 (version 6.0.6002). Use pip to install with this version of Windows.

2. Run the downloaded MSI installer.

3. Follow the instructions that appear.

The CLI installs to `C:\Program Files\Amazon\AWSCLI` (64-bit) or `C:\Program Files (x86)\Amazon\AWSCLI` (32-bit) by default. To confirm the installation, use the `aws --version` command at a command prompt (open the START menu and search for "cmd" if you're not sure where the command prompt is installed).

```
1 > aws --version
2 aws-cli/1.11.84 Python/3.6.2 Windows/7 botocore/1.5.47
```

Don't include the prompt symbol ('>' above) when you type a command. These are included in program listings to differentiate commands that you type from output returned by the CLI. The rest of this guide uses the generic prompt symbol '$' except in cases where a command is Windows-specific.

If Windows is unable to find the executable, you may need to re-open the command prompt or add the installation directory to your PATH environment variable manually.

Updating an MSI Installation

The AWS CLI is updated regularly. Check out the Releases page on GitHub to see when the latest version was released. To update to the latest version, download and run the MSI installer again as detailed above.

Uninstalling

To uninstall the AWS CLI, open the Control Panel and select *Programs and Features*. Select the entry named *AWS Command Line Interface* and click *Uninstall* to launch the uninstaller. Confirm that you wish to uninstall the AWS CLI when prompted.

You can also launch the *Programs and Features* menu from the command line with the following command:

```
1 > appwiz.cpl
```

Install Python, pip, and the AWS CLI on Windows

The Python Software Foundation provides installers for Windows that include `pip`.

To install Python 3.6 and pip (Windows)

1. Download the Python 3.6 Windows x86-64 executable installer from the downloads page of Python.org.

2. Run the installer.

3. Choose **Add Python 3.6 to PATH**.

4. Choose **Install Now**.

The installer installs Python in your user folder and adds its executable directories to your user path.

To install the AWS CLI with pip (Windows)

1. Open the Windows Command Processor from the Start menu.

2. Verify that Python and pip are both installed correctly with the following commands:

```
1 C:\Windows\System32> python --version
2 Python 3.6.2
3 C:\Windows\System32> pip --version
4 pip 9.0.1 from c:\users\myname\appdata\local\programs\python\python36\lib\site-packages (
    python 3.6)
```

3. Install the AWS CLI using `pip`:

```
1 C:\Windows\System32> pip install awscli
```

4. Verify that the AWS CLI is installed correctly:

```
1 C:\Windows\System32> aws --version
2 aws-cli/1.11.84 Python/3.6.2 Windows/7 botocore/1.5.47
```

To upgrade to the latest version, run the installation command again:

```
1 C:\Windows\System32> pip install --user --upgrade awscli
```

Adding the AWS CLI Executable to your Command Line Path

After installing with `pip`, add the `aws` executable to your OS's `PATH` environment variable. With an MSI installation, this should happen automatically, but you may need to set it manually if the `aws` command is not working.

- **Python 3.6 and pip** – `%USERPROFILE%\AppData\Local\Programs\Python\Python36\Scripts`
- **MSI installer (64-bit)** – `C:\Program Files\Amazon\AWSCLI`
- **MSI installer (32-bit)** – `C:\Program Files (x86)\Amazon\AWSCLI`

To modify your PATH variable (Windows)

1. Press the Windows key and type **environment variables**.

2. Choose **Edit environment variables for your account**.

3. Choose **PATH** and then choose **Edit**.

18

4. Add paths to the **Variable value** field, separated by semicolons. For example: `C:\existing\path;C:\new\path`

5. Choose **OK** twice to apply the new settings.

6. Close any running command prompts and re-open.

Install the AWS Command Line Interface on macOS

If you have pip, follow the instructions in the main installation topic. Run `pip --version` to see if your version of macOS already includes Python and pip.

```
1 $ pip --version
```

- Install Python, pip, and the AWS CLI on macOS
- Adding the AWS CLI Executable to your Command Line Path

Install Python, pip, and the AWS CLI on macOS

You can install the latest version of Python and pip and then use them to install the AWS CLI.

To install the AWS CLI on macOS

1. Download and install Python 3.6 from the downloads page of Python.org.

2. Install `pip` with the script provided by the Python Packaging Authority.

```
1 $ curl -O https://bootstrap.pypa.io/get-pip.py
2 $ python3 get-pip.py --user
```

3. Use `pip` to install the AWS CLI.

```
1 $ pip3 install awscli --upgrade --user
```

4. Verify that the AWS CLI is installed correctly.

```
1 $ aws --version
2 AWS CLI 1.11.84 (Python 3.6.1)
```

   If the executable is not found, add it to your command line path.

To upgrade to the latest version, run the installation command again:

```
1 $ pip3 install awscli --upgrade --user
```

Adding the AWS CLI Executable to your Command Line Path

After installing with `pip`, you may need to add the `aws` executable to your OS's `PATH` environment variable. The location of the executable depends on where Python is installed.

Example AWS CLI install location - macOS with Python 3.6 and pip (user mode)

```
1 ~/Library/Python/3.6/bin
```

If you don't know where Python is installed, run `which python`.

```
1 $ which python
2 /usr/local/bin/python
```

The output may be the path to a symlink, not the actual executable. Run `ls -al` to see where it points.

```
1 $ ls -al /usr/local/bin/python
2 ~/Library/Python/3.6/bin/python3.6
```

`pip` installs executables to the same folder that contains the Python executable. Add this folder to your PATH variable.

To modify your PATH variable (Linux, macOS, or Unix)

1. Find your shell's profile script in your user folder. If you are not sure which shell you have, run `echo $SHELL`.

```
1 $ ls -a ~
2 .  ..  .bash_logout  .bash_profile  .bashrc  Desktop  Documents  Downloads
```

   - **Bash** – `.bash_profile`, `.profile`, or `.bash_login`.
   - **Zsh** – `.zshrc`
   - **Tcsh** – `.tcshrc`, `.cshrc` or `.login`.

2. Add an export command to your profile script.

```
1 export PATH=~/.local/bin:$PATH
```

   This command adds a path, `~/.local/bin` in this example, to the current PATH variable.

3. Load the profile into your current session.

```
1 $ source ~/.bash_profile
```

Install the AWS Command Line Interface in a Virtual Environment

You can avoid requirement version conflicts with other pip packages by installing the AWS CLI in a virtual environment.

To install the AWS CLI in a virtual environment

1. Install `virtualenv` with pip.

```
1 $ pip install --user virtualenv
```

2. Create a virtual environment.

```
1 $ virtualenv ~/cli-ve
```

   You can use the -p option to use a Python executable other than the default.

```
1 $ virtualenv -p /usr/bin/python3.4 ~/cli-ve
```

3. Activate the virtual environment.

   Linux, macOS, or Unix

```
1 $ source ~/cli-ve/bin/activate
```

   Windows

```
1 $ %USERPROFILE%\cli-ve\Scripts\activate
```

4. Install the AWS CLI.

```
1 (cli-ve)~$ pip install --upgrade awscli
```

5. Verify that the AWS CLI is installed correctly.

```
1 $ aws --version
2 aws-cli/1.11.84 Python/3.6.2 Linux/4.4.0-59-generic botocore/1.5.47
```

You can use the `deactivate` command to exit the virtual environment. Whenever you start a new session, run the activation command again.

To upgrade to the latest version, run the installation command again:

```
1 (cli-ve)~$ pip install --upgrade awscli
```

Install the AWS CLI Using the Bundled Installer (Linux, macOS, or Unix)

On Linux, macOS, or Unix, you can also use the bundled installer to install the AWS CLI. The bundled installer includes all dependencies and can be used offline.

Important
The bundled installer does not support installing to paths that contain spaces.

- Prerequisites
- Install the AWS CLI Using the Bundled Installer
- Install the AWS CLI Without Sudo (Linux, macOS, or Unix)
- Uninstalling

Prerequisites

- Linux, macOS, or Unix

- Python 2 version 2.6.5+ or Python 3 version 3.3+

Check your Python installation:

```
1 $ python --version
```

If your computer doesn't already have Python installed, or you would like to install a different version of Python, follow the procedure in .

Install the AWS CLI Using the Bundled Installer

Follow these steps from the command line to install the AWS CLI using the bundled installer.

To install the AWS CLI using the bundled installer

1. Download the AWS CLI Bundled Installer.

```
1 $ curl "https://s3.amazonaws.com/aws-cli/awscli-bundle.zip" -o "awscli-bundle.zip"
```

2. Unzip the package.

```
1 $ unzip awscli-bundle.zip
```

Note
If you don't have `unzip`, use your Linux distribution's built in package manager to install it.

1. Run the install executable.

```
1 $ sudo ./awscli-bundle/install -i /usr/local/aws -b /usr/local/bin/aws
```

Note
By default, the install script runs under the system default version of Python. If you have installed an alternative version of Python and want to use that to install the AWS CLI, run the install script with that version by absolute path to the Python executable. For example:

```
1 $ sudo /usr/local/bin/python2.7 awscli-bundle/install -i /usr/local/aws -b /usr/local/bin/aws
```

The installer installs the AWS CLI at `/usr/local/aws` and creates the symlink `aws` at the `/usr/local/bin` directory. Using the `-b` option to create a symlink eliminates the need to specify the install directory in the user's `$PATH` variable. This should enable all users to call the AWS CLI by typing `aws` from any directory.

To see an explanation of the `-i` and `-b` options, use the `-h` option:

```
1 $ ./awscli-bundle/install -h
```

Install the AWS CLI Without Sudo (Linux, macOS, or Unix)

If you don't have sudo permissions or want to install the AWS CLI only for the current user, you can use a modified version of the above commands:

```
1 $ curl "https://s3.amazonaws.com/aws-cli/awscli-bundle.zip" -o "awscli-bundle.zip"
2 $ unzip awscli-bundle.zip
3 $ ./awscli-bundle/install -b ~/bin/aws
```

This installs the AWS CLI to the default location (`~/.local/lib/aws`) and create a symbolic link (symlink) at `~/bin/aws`. Make sure that `~/bin` is in your `PATH` environment variable for the symlink to work:

```
1 $ echo $PATH | grep ~/bin     // See if $PATH contains ~/bin (output will be empty if it doesn't
    )
2 $ export PATH=~/bin:$PATH     // Add ~/bin to $PATH if necessary
```

Tip
To ensure that your $PATH settings are retained between sessions, add the `export` line to your shell profile (~/.profile, ~/.bash_profile, etc).

Uninstalling

The bundled installer does not put anything outside of the installation directory except the optional symlink, so uninstalling is as simple as deleting those two items.

```
1 $ sudo rm -rf /usr/local/aws
2 $ sudo rm /usr/local/bin/aws
```

Configuring the AWS CLI

This section explains how to configure settings that the AWS Command Line Interface uses when interacting with AWS, such as your security credentials and the default region.

Note
The AWS CLI signs requests on your behalf, and includes a date in the signature. Ensure that your computer's date and time are set correctly; if not, the date in the signature may not match the date of the request, and AWS rejects the request.

- Quick Configuration
- Configuration Settings and Precedence
- Configuration and Credential Files
- Named Profiles
- Environment Variables
- Command Line Options
- Instance Metadata
- Using an HTTP Proxy
- Assuming a Role
- Command Completion

Quick Configuration

For general use, the `aws configure` command is the fastest way to set up your AWS CLI installation.

```
1 $ aws configure
2 AWS Access Key ID [None]: AKIAIOSFODNN7EXAMPLE
3 AWS Secret Access Key [None]: wJalrXUtnFEMI/K7MDENG/bPxRfiCYEXAMPLEKEY
4 Default region name [None]: us-west-2
5 Default output format [None]: json
```

The AWS CLI will prompt you for four pieces of information. AWS Access Key ID and AWS Secret Access Key are your account credentials.

To get the access key ID and secret access key for an IAM user

Access keys consist of an access key ID and secret access key, which are used to sign programmatic requests that you make to AWS. If you don't have access keys, you can create them from the AWS Management Console. We recommend that you use IAM access keys instead of AWS account root user access keys. IAM lets you securely control access to AWS services and resources in your AWS account.

The only time that you can view or download the secret access keys is when you create the keys. You cannot recover them later. However, you can create new access keys at any time. You must also have permissions to perform the required IAM actions. For more information, see Permissions Required to Access IAM Resources in the *IAM User Guide.*

1. Open the IAM console.

2. In the navigation pane of the console, choose **Users**.

3. Choose your IAM user name (not the check box).

4. Choose the **Security credentials** tab and then choose **Create access key**.

5. To see the new access key, choose **Show**. Your credentials will look something like this:

   - Access key ID: AKIAIOSFODNN7EXAMPLE

   - Secret access key: wJalrXUtnFEMI/K7MDENG/bPxRfiCYEXAMPLEKEY

6. To download the key pair, choose **Download .csv file**. Store the keys in a secure location.

   Keep the keys confidential in order to protect your AWS account, and never email them. Do not share them outside your organization, even if an inquiry appears to come from AWS or Amazon.com. No one who legitimately represents Amazon will ever ask you for your secret key.

Related topics

- What Is IAM? in the *IAM User Guide*

- AWS Security Credentials in *AWS General Reference*

Default region is the name of the region you want to make calls against by default. This is usually the region closest to you, but it can be any region. For example, type `us-west-2` to use US West (Oregon).

Note

You must specify an AWS region when using the AWS CLI. For a list of services and available regions, see Regions and Endpoints. The region designators used by the AWS CLI are the same names that you see in AWS Management Console URLs and service endpoints.

Default output format can be either `json`, `text`, or `table`. If you don't specify an output format, `json` is used.

If you have multiple profiles, you can configure additional, named profiles by using the `--profile` option.

```
1 $ aws configure --profile user2
2 AWS Access Key ID [None]: AKIAI44QH8DHBEXAMPLE
3 AWS Secret Access Key [None]: je7MtGbClwBF/2Zp9Utk/h3yCo8nvbEXAMPLEKEY
4 Default region name [None]: us-east-1
5 Default output format [None]: text
```

To update any of your settings, simply run `aws configure` again and enter new values as appropriate. The next sections contain more information on the files that `aws configure` creates, additional settings, and named profiles.

Configuration Settings and Precedence

The AWS CLI uses a *provider chain* to look for AWS credentials in a number of different places, including system or user environment variables and local AWS configuration files.

The AWS CLI looks for credentials and configuration settings in the following order:

1. **Command line options** – region, output format and profile can be specified as command options to override default settings.

2. **Environment variables** – `AWS_ACCESS_KEY_ID`, `AWS_SECRET_ACCESS_KEY`, and `AWS_SESSION_TOKEN`.

3. **The AWS credentials file** – located at `~/.aws/credentials` on Linux, macOS, or Unix, or at `C:\Users\USERNAME\.aws\credentials` on Windows. This file can contain multiple named profiles in addition to a default profile.

4. **The CLI configuration file** – typically located at `~/.aws/config` on Linux, macOS, or Unix, or at `C:\Users\USERNAME\.aws\config` on Windows. This file can contain a default profile, named profiles, and CLI specific configuration parameters for each.

5. **Container credentials** – provided by Amazon Elastic Container Service on container instances when you assign a role to your task.

6. **Instance profile credentials** – these credentials can be used on EC2 instances with an assigned instance role, and are delivered through the Amazon EC2 metadata service.

Configuration and Credential Files

The CLI stores credentials specified with `aws configure` in a local file named `credentials` in a folder named `.aws` in your home directory. Home directory location varies but can be referred to using the environment variables `%UserProfile%` in Windows and `$HOME` or ~ (tilde) in Unix-like systems.

For example, the following commands list the contents of the `.aws` folder:

Linux, macOS, or Unix

```
1 $ ls  ~/.aws
```

Windows

```
1 > dir "%UserProfile%\.aws"
```

In order to separate credentials from less sensitive options, region and output format are stored in a separate file named `config` in the same folder.

The default file location for the config file can be overridden by setting the AWS_CONFIG_FILE environment variable to another local path. See for details.

Storing Credentials in Config

The AWS CLI will also read credentials from the config file. If you want to keep all of your profile settings in a single file, you can. If there are ever credentials in both locations for a profile (say you used `aws configure` to update the profile's keys), the keys in the credentials file will take precedence.

If you use one of the SDKs in addition to the AWS CLI, you may notice additional warnings if credentials are not stored in their own file.

The files generated by the CLI for the profile configured in the previous section look like this:

~/.aws/credentials

```
1 [default]
2 aws_access_key_id=AKIAIOSFODNN7EXAMPLE
3 aws_secret_access_key=wJalrXUtnFEMI/K7MDENG/bPxRfiCYEXAMPLEKEY
```

~/.aws/config

```
1 [default]
2 region=us-west-2
3 output=json
```

The following settings are supported.

aws_access_key_id – AWS access key.

aws_secret_access_key – AWS secret key.

aws_session_token – AWS session token. A session token is only required if you are using temporary security credentials.

region – AWS region.

output – output format (json, text, or table)

Named Profiles

The AWS CLI supports *named profiles* stored in the config and credentials files. You can configure additional profiles by using `aws configure` with the `--profile` option or by adding entries to the config and credentials files.

The following example shows a credentials file with two profiles:

~/.aws/credentials

```
1 [default]
2 aws_access_key_id=AKIAIOSFODNN7EXAMPLE
3 aws_secret_access_key=wJalrXUtnFEMI/K7MDENG/bPxRfiCYEXAMPLEKEY
4
5 [user2]
6 aws_access_key_id=AKIAI44QH8DHBEXAMPLE
7 aws_secret_access_key=je7MtGbClwBF/2Zp9Utk/h3yCo8nvbEXAMPLEKEY
```

Each profile uses different credentials—perhaps from two different IAM users—and can also use different regions and output formats.

~/.aws/config

```
1 [default]
2 region=us-west-2
3 output=json
4
5 [profile user2]
6 region=us-east-1
7 output=text
```

Important
The AWS credentials file uses a different naming format than the CLI config file for named profiles. Do not include the 'profile ' prefix when configuring a named profile in the AWS credentials file.

Using Profiles with the AWS CLI

To use a named profile, add the `--profile` option to your command. The following example lists running instances using the `user2` profile from the previous section.

```
1 $ aws ec2 describe-instances --profile user2
```

If you are going to use a named profile for multiple commands, you can avoid specifying the profile in every command by setting the AWS_PROFILE environment variable at the command line:

Linux, macOS, or Unix

```
1 $ export AWS_PROFILE=user2
```

Windows

```
1 > set AWS_PROFILE=user2
```

Setting the environment variable changes the default profile until the end of your shell session, or until you set the variable to a different value. More on variables in the next section.

Environment Variables

Environment variables override configuration and credential files and can be useful for scripting or temporarily setting a named profile as the default.

The AWS CLI supports the following environment variables.

- `AWS_ACCESS_KEY_ID` – AWS access key.

- `AWS_SECRET_ACCESS_KEY` – AWS secret key. Access and secret key variables override credentials stored in credential and config files.

- `AWS_SESSION_TOKEN` – Specify a session token if you are using temporary security credentials.

- `AWS_DEFAULT_REGION` – AWS region. This variable overrides the default region of the in-use profile, if set.

- `AWS_DEFAULT_OUTPUT` – Change the AWS CLI's output formatting to `json`, `text`, or `table`.

- `AWS_PROFILE` – name of the CLI profile to use. This can be the name of a profile stored in a credential or config file, or `default` to use the default profile.

- `AWS_CA_BUNDLE` – Specify the path to a certificate bundle to use for HTTPS certificate validation.

- `AWS_SHARED_CREDENTIALS_FILE` – Change the location of the file that the AWS CLI uses to store access keys.

- `AWS_CONFIG_FILE` – Change the location of the file that the AWS CLI uses to store configuration profiles.

The following example shows how you would configure environment variables for the default user from earlier in this guide.

Linux, macOS, or Unix

```
1 $ export AWS_ACCESS_KEY_ID=AKIAIOSFODNN7EXAMPLE
2 $ export AWS_SECRET_ACCESS_KEY=wJalrXUtnFEMI/K7MDENG/bPxRfiCYEXAMPLEKEY
3 $ export AWS_DEFAULT_REGION=us-west-2
```

Windows

```
1 > set AWS_ACCESS_KEY_ID=AKIAIOSFODNN7EXAMPLE
2 > set AWS_SECRET_ACCESS_KEY=wJalrXUtnFEMI/K7MDENG/bPxRfiCYEXAMPLEKEY
3 > set AWS_DEFAULT_REGION=us-west-2
```

Command Line Options

The AWS CLI uses GNU-style long command line options preceded by two hyphens. Command line options can be used to override default configuration settings for a single operation, but cannot be used to specify credentials.

The following settings can be specified at the command line.

--profile – name of a profile to use, or "default" to use the default profile.

--region – AWS region to call.

--output – output format.

--endpoint-url – The endpoint to make the call against. The endpoint can be the address of a proxy or an endpoint URL for the in-use AWS region. Specifying an endpoint is not required for normal use as the AWS CLI determines which endpoint to call based on the in-use region.

The above options override the corresponding profile settings for a single operation. Each takes a string argument with a space or equals sign ("=") separating the argument from the option name. Quotes around the argument are not required unless the argument string contains a space.

Tip
You can use the --profile option with `aws configure` to set up additional profiles

```
1 $ aws configure --profile profilename
```

Common uses for command line options include checking your resources in multiple regions and changing output format for legibility or ease of use when scripting. For example, if you are not sure which region your instance is running in you could run the describe-instances command against each region until you find it:

```
 1 $ aws ec2 describe-instances --output table --region us-east-1
 2 -------------------
 3 |DescribeInstances|
 4 +-----------------+
 5 $ aws ec2 describe-instances --output table --region us-west-1
 6 -------------------
 7 |DescribeInstances|
 8 +-----------------+
 9 $ aws ec2 describe-instances --output table --region us-west-2
10 -----------------------------------------------------------------------
11 |                         DescribeInstances                           |
12 +---------------------------------------------------------------------+
13 ||                           Reservations                            ||
14 |+-----------------------------------+-------------------------------+|
15 ||  OwnerId                          |  012345678901                 ||
16 ||  ReservationId                    |  r-abcdefgh                   ||
17 |+-----------------------------------+-------------------------------+|
18 |||                           Instances                            |||
19 ||+-----------------------+---------------------------------------+||
20 |||  AmiLaunchIndex       |  0                                     |||
21 |||  Architecture         |  x86_64                                |||
22 ...
```

Command line option parameter types (string, boolean, etc.) are discussed in detail in the section later in this guide.

Instance Metadata

To use the CLI from an EC2 instance, create a role that has access to the resources needed and assign that role to the instance when it is launched. Launch the instance and check to see if the AWS CLI is already installed (it comes pre-installed on Amazon Linux).

Install the AWS CLI if necessary and configure a default region to avoid having to specify it in every command. You can set the region using `aws configure` without entering credentials by pressing enter twice to skip the first two prompts:

```
1 $ aws configure
2 AWS Access Key ID [None]: ENTER
3 AWS Secret Access Key [None]: ENTER
4 Default region name [None]: us-west-2
5 Default output format [None]: json
```

The AWS CLI will read credentials from the instance metadata. For more information, see Granting Applications that Run on Amazon EC2 Instances Access to AWS Resources in *IAM User Guide*.

Using an HTTP Proxy

If you need to access AWS through proxy servers, you should configure the `HTTP_PROXY` and `HTTPS_PROXY` environment variables with the IP addresses for your proxy servers.

Linux, macOS, or Unix

```
1 $ export HTTP_PROXY=http://a.b.c.d:n
2 $ export HTTPS_PROXY=http://w.x.y.z:m
```

Windows

```
1 > set HTTP_PROXY=http://a.b.c.d:n
2 > set HTTPS_PROXY=http://w.x.y.z:m
```

In these examples, `http://a.b.c.d:n` and `http://w.x.y.z:m` are the IP addresses and ports for the HTTP and HTTPS proxies.

Authenticating to a Proxy

The AWS CLI supports HTTP Basic authentication. Specify a username and password in the proxy URL like this:

Linux, macOS, or Unix

```
1 $ export HTTP_PROXY=http://username:password@a.b.c.d:n
2 $ export HTTPS_PROXY=http://username:password@w.x.y.z:m
```

Windows

```
1 > set HTTP_PROXY=http://username:password@a.b.c.d:n
2 > set HTTPS_PROXY=http://username:password@w.x.y.z:m
```

Note
The AWS CLI does not support NTLM proxies. If you use an NTLM or Kerberos proxy, you may be able to connect through an authentication proxy like Cntlm.

Using a proxy on EC2 Instances

If you configure a proxy on an ec2 instance launched with an IAM role, you should also set the `NO_PROXY` environment variable with the IP address 169.254.169.254, so that the AWS CLI can access the Instance Meta Data Service (IMDS).

Linux, macOS, or Unix

```
1 $ export NO_PROXY=169.254.169.254
```

Windows

```
1 > set NO_PROXY=169.254.169.254
```

Assuming a Role

An IAM role is a authorization tool that lets a user gain additional permissions, or get permission to perform actions in a different account.

You can configure the AWS Command Line Interface to use a role by creating a profile for the role in the `~/.aws/config` file. The following example shows a role profile named `marketingadmin` that is assumed by the default profile.

```
1 [profile marketingadmin]
2 role_arn = arn:aws:iam::123456789012:role/marketingadmin
3 source_profile = default
```

In this case, the default profile is an IAM user with credentials and permission to assume a role named marketingadmin. To access the role, you create a named profile. Instead of configuring this profile with credentials, you specify the ARN of the role and the name of the profile that has access to it.

- Configuring and Using a Role
- Using Multifactor Authentication
- Cross Account Roles
- Clearing Cached Credentials

Configuring and Using a Role

When you run commands using the role profile, the AWS CLI uses the source profile's credentials to call AWS Security Token Service and assume the specified role. The source profile must have permission to call `sts:assume-role` against the role, and the role must have a trust relationship with the source profile to allow itself to be assumed.

Create a new role in IAM with the permissions that you want users to assume by following the procedure under Creating a Role to Delegate Permissions to an IAM User in the *AWS Identity and Access Management User Guide*. If the role and the target IAM user are in the same account, you can enter your own account ID when configuring the role's trust relationship.

After creating the role, modify the trust relationship to allow the IAM user to assume it. The following example shows a trust relationship that allows a role to be assumed by an IAM user named `jonsmith`:

```
1  {
2    "Version": "2012-10-17",
3    "Statement": [
4      {
5        "Sid": "",
6        "Effect": "Allow",
7        "Principal": {
8          "AWS": "arn:aws:iam::123456789012:user/jonsmith"
9        },
10       "Action": "sts:AssumeRole"
11     }
12   ]
13 }
```

Next, grant your IAM user permission to assume the role. The following example shows an AWS Identity and Access Management policy that allows an IAM user to assume the `marketingadmin` role:

```
1  {
2    "Version": "2012-10-17",
3    "Statement": [
```

```
4     {
5        "Effect": "Allow",
6        "Action": "sts:AssumeRole",
7        "Resource": "arn:aws:iam::123456789012:role/marketingadmin"
8     }
9   ]
10 }
```

The user doesn't need to have any additional permissions to run commands using the role profile. If you want your users to be able to access AWS resources without using the role, apply additional inline or managed policies for those resources.

With the role profile, role permissions, trust relationship and user permissions applied, you can assume the role at the command line by using the `profile` option, for example:

```
1 $ aws s3 ls --profile marketingadmin
```

To use the role for multiple calls, you can set the AWS_PROFILE environment variable for the current session from the command line:

Linux, macOS, or Unix

```
1 $ export AWS_PROFILE=marketingadmin
```

Windows

```
1 > set AWS_PROFILE=marketingadmin
```

For more information on configuring IAM users and roles, see Users and Groups and Roles in the *AWS Identity and Access Management User Guide*.

Using Multifactor Authentication

For additional security, you can require users to provide a one time key generated from a multifactor authentication device or mobile app when they attempt to make a call using the role profile.

First, modify the trust relationship on the role to require multifactor authentication:

```
1  {
2    "Version": "2012-10-17",
3    "Statement": [
4      {
5        "Sid": "",
6        "Effect": "Allow",
7        "Principal": { "AWS": "arn:aws:iam::123456789012:user/jonsmith" },
8        "Action": "sts:AssumeRole",
9        "Condition": { "Bool": { "aws:MultiFactorAuthPresent": true } }
10     }
11   ]
12 }
```

Next, add a line to the role profile that specifies the ARN of the user's MFA device:

```
1 [profile marketingadmin]
2 role_arn = arn:aws:iam::123456789012:role/marketingadmin
3 source_profile = default
4 mfa_serial = arn:aws:iam::123456789012:mfa/jonsmith
```

The `mfa_serial` setting can take an ARN, as shown, or the serial number of a hardware MFA token.

Cross Account Roles

You can enable IAM users to assume roles that belong to different accounts by configuring the role as a cross account role. During role creation, set the role type to one of the options under **Role for Cross-Account Access** and optionally select **Require MFA**. The **Require MFA** option configures the appropriate condition in the trust relationship as described in .

If you use an external ID to provide additional control over who can assume a role across accounts, add an `external_id` parameter to the role profile:

```
1 [profile crossaccountrole]
2 role_arn = arn:aws:iam::234567890123:role/xaccount
3 source_profile = default
4 mfa_serial = arn:aws:iam::123456789012:mfa/jonsmith
5 external_id = 123456
```

Clearing Cached Credentials

When you assume a role, the AWS CLI caches the temporary credentials locally until they expire. If your role's temporary credentials are revoked, you can delete the cache to force the AWS CLI to retrieve new credentials.

Linux, macOS, or Unix

```
1 $ rm -r ~/.aws/cli/cache
```

Windows

```
1 > del /s /q %UserProfile%\.aws\cli\cache
```

Command Completion

On Unix-like systems, the AWS CLI includes a command-completion feature that enables you to use the TAB key to complete a partially typed command. This feature is not automatically installed so you need to configure it manually.

Configuring command completion requires two pieces of information: the name of the shell you are using and the location of the aws_completer script.

Completion on Amazon Linux
Command completion is configured by default on instances running Amazon Linux.

- Identify Your Shell
- Locate the AWS Completer
- Enable Command Completion
- Test Command Completion

Identify Your Shell

If you are not sure which shell you are using, identify it with one of the following commands:

echo $SHELL – show the shell's installation directory. This will usually match the in-use shell, unless you launched a different shell after logging in.

```
1 $ echo $SHELL
2 /bin/bash
```

ps – show the processes running for the current user. The shell will be one of them.

```
1 $ ps
2   PID TTY          TIME CMD
3  2148 pts/1     00:00:00 bash
4  8756 pts/1     00:00:00 ps
```

Locate the AWS Completer

The location can vary depending on the installation method used.

Package Manager – programs such as pip, yum, brew and apt-get typically install the AWS completer (or a symlink to it) to a standard path location. In this case, `which` will locate the completer for you.

```
1 $ which aws_completer
2 /usr/local/bin/aws_completer
```

Bundled Installer – if you used the bundled installer per the instructions in the previous section, the AWS completer will be located in the bin subfolder of the installation directory.

```
1 $ ls /usr/local/aws/bin
2 activate
3 activate.csh
4 activate.fish
5 activate_this.py
6 aws
7 aws.cmd
8 aws_completer
9 ...
```

If all else fails, you can use **find** to search your entire file system for the AWS completer.

```
1 $ find / -name aws_completer
2 /usr/local/aws/bin/aws_completer
```

Enable Command Completion

Run a command to enable command completion. The command that you use to enable completion depends on the shell that you are using. You can add the command to your shell's RC file to run it each time you open a new shell.

- **bash** – use the built-in command `complete`.

```
1 $ complete -C '/usr/local/bin/aws_completer' aws
```

  Add the command to `~/.bashrc` to run it each time you open a new shell. Your `~/.bash_profile` should source `~/.bashrc` to ensure that the command is run in login shells as well.

- **tcsh** – complete for tcsh takes a word type and pattern to define the completion behavior.

```
1 > complete aws 'p/*/`aws_completer`/'
```

Add the command to `~/.tschrc` to run it each time you open a new shell.

- **zsh** – source `bin/aws_zsh_completer.sh`.

```
1 % source /usr/local/bin/aws_zsh_completer.sh
```

The AWS CLI uses bash compatibility auto completion (`bashcompinit`) for zsh support. For further details, refer to the top of `aws_zsh_completer.sh`.

Add the command to `~/.zshrc` to run it each time you open a new shell.

Test Command Completion

After enabling command completion, type in a partial command and press tab to see the available commands.

```
1 $ aws sTAB
2 s3           ses           sqs            sts        swf
3 s3api        sns           storagegateway support
```

Deploying a Development Environment in Amazon EC2 Using the AWS Command Line Interface

This tutorial details how to set up a development environment in Amazon EC2 using the AWS CLI. It includes a short version of the installation and configuration instructions, and it can be run start to finish on Windows, Linux, macOS, or Unix.

- Install the AWS CLI
- Configure the AWS CLI
- Create a Security Group, Key Pair, and Role for the EC2 Instance
- Launch and Connect to the Instance

Install the AWS CLI

You can install the AWS CLI with an installer (Windows) or by using `pip`, a package manager for Python.

Windows

1. Download the MSI installer.

   - Download the AWS CLI MSI installer for Windows (64-bit)

   - Download the AWS CLI MSI installer for Windows (32-bit)

2. Run the downloaded MSI installer.

3. Follow the instructions that appear.

Linux, macOS, or Unix

These steps require that you have a working installation of Python 2 version 2.6.5+ or Python 3 version 3.3+. If you encounter any issues using the following steps, see the full installation instructions in the AWS Command Line Interface User Guide.

1. Download and run the installation script from the pip website:

   ```
   1 $ curl "https://bootstrap.pypa.io/get-pip.py" -o "get-pip.py"
   2 $ python get-pip.py --user
   ```

2. Install the AWS CLI Using `pip`:

   ```
   1 $ pip install awscli --user
   ```

Configure the AWS CLI

Run `aws configure` at the command line to set up your credentials and settings.

```
1 $ aws configure
2 AWS Access Key ID [None]: AKIAIOSFODNN7EXAMPLE
3 AWS Secret Access Key [None]: wJalrXUtnFEMI/K7MDENG/bPxRfiCYEXAMPLEKEY
4 Default region name [None]: us-west-2
5 Default output format [None]: json
```

The AWS CLI will prompt you for the following information:

- **AWS Access Key ID and AWS Secret Access Key** – These are your account credentials. If you don't have keys, see How Do I Get Security Credentials? in the *Amazon Web Services General Reference*.

- **Default region name** – This is the name of the region you want to make calls against by default. **Note** Use `us-west-2` for this tutorial (the AMI we will use is specific to this region). You can change the default region later by running `aws configure` again.

- **Default output format** – This format can be either json, text, or table. If you don't specify an output format, json will be used.

Run a command to verify that your credentials are configured correctly and that you can connect to AWS.

```
$ aws ec2 describe-regions --output table
-------------------------------------------------------
|                    DescribeRegions                  |
+-----------------------------------------------------+
||                      Regions                      ||
|+-----------------------------------+---------------+|
||              Endpoint             |  RegionName   ||
|+-----------------------------------+---------------+|
||  ec2.ap-south-1.amazonaws.com     |  ap-south-1   ||
||  ec2.eu-west-2.amazonaws.com      |  eu-west-2    ||
||  ec2.eu-west-1.amazonaws.com      |  eu-west-1    ||
||  ec2.ap-northeast-2.amazonaws.com |  ap-northeast-2 ||
||  ec2.ap-northeast-1.amazonaws.com |  ap-northeast-1 ||
||  ec2.sa-east-1.amazonaws.com      |  sa-east-1    ||
||  ec2.ca-central-1.amazonaws.com   |  ca-central-1 ||
||  ec2.ap-southeast-1.amazonaws.com |  ap-southeast-1 ||
||  ec2.ap-southeast-2.amazonaws.com |  ap-southeast-2 ||
||  ec2.eu-central-1.amazonaws.com   |  eu-central-1 ||
||  ec2.us-east-1.amazonaws.com      |  us-east-1    ||
||  ec2.us-east-2.amazonaws.com      |  us-east-2    ||
||  ec2.us-west-1.amazonaws.com      |  us-west-1    ||
||  ec2.us-west-2.amazonaws.com      |  us-west-2    ||
|+-----------------------------------+---------------+|
```

Create a Security Group, Key Pair, and Role for the EC2 Instance

Your next step is to set up prerequisites for launching an EC2 instance that can be accessed using SSH. For more information about Amazon EC2 features, go to the *Amazon EC2 User Guide for Linux Instances*

To create a security group, key pair, and role

1. First, create a new security group and add a rule that allows incoming traffic over port 22 for SSH. Note the security group ID for later use.

```
$ aws ec2 create-security-group --group-name devenv-sg --description "security group for
    development environment in EC2"
{
    "GroupId": "sg-b018ced5"
}
$ aws ec2 authorize-security-group-ingress --group-name devenv-sg --protocol tcp --port 22
    --cidr 0.0.0.0/0
```

2. Replace the CIDR range in the above with the one that you will connect from for more security. You can use the `aws ec2 describe-security-groups` command to admire your handiwork.

3. Next, create a key pair, which allows you to connect to the instance.

```
1 $ aws ec2 create-key-pair --key-name devenv-key --query 'KeyMaterial' --output text >
    devenv-key.pem
```

This command saves the contents of the key to a file called `devenv-key.pem`. **Windows**
In the Windows Command Processor, enclose queries with double quotes instead of single quotes.

4. On Linux, you will also need to change the file mode so that only you have access to the key file.

```
1 $ chmod 400 devenv-key.pem
```

Launch and Connect to the Instance

Finally, you are ready to launch an instance and connect to it.

To launch and connect to the instance

1. Run the following command, replacing the security group ID output in the previous step.

```
1 $ aws ec2 run-instances --image-id ami-6e1a0117 --security-group-ids sg-b018ced5 --count 1
    --instance-type t2.micro --key-name devenv-key --query 'Instances[0].InstanceId'
2 "i-0787e4282810ef9cf"
```

The image ID *ami-6e1a0117* specifies the Amazon Machine Image (AMI) that Amazon EC2 uses to bootstrap the instance. You can find image IDs for other regions and operating systems in the Amazon EC2 Management Console Launch Instance Wizard. **Note**
T2 instance types require a VPC. If you don't have a default VPC, you can specify a subnet in a custom VPC with the `--subnet-id` option. If you don't have any VPCs, choose a different instance type such as `t1.micro`.

2. The instance will take a few moments to launch. Once the instance is up and running, the following command will retrieve the public IP address that you will use to connect to the instance.

```
1 $ aws ec2 describe-instances --instance-ids "i-0787e4282810ef9cf" --query 'Reservations[0].
    Instances[0].PublicIpAddress'
2 "54.183.22.255"
```

3. To connect to the instance, use the public IP address and private key with your preferred terminal program. On Linux, macOS, or Unix, you can do this from the command line with the following command:

```
1 $ ssh -i devenv-key.pem ubuntu@54.183.22.255
```

If you get an error like *Permission denied (publickey)* when attempting to connect to your instance, check that the following are correct:

- **Key** – The key specified with the `-i` option must be at the path indicated and must be the private key, not the public one. Permissions on the key must be restricted to the owner.

- **User name** – The user name must match the user associated with the key pair on the instance. For Ubuntu instances, this is `ubuntu`. For Amazon Linux, it is `ec2-user`.

- **Instance** – The public IP address or DNS name of the instance. Verify that the address is public and that port 22 is open to your local machine on the instance's security group.

You can also use the `-v` option to view additional information related to the error. **SSH on Windows**
On Windows, you can use the PuTTY terminal application available here. Get `putty.exe` and `puttygen.exe` from the downloads page.
Use `puttygen.exe` to convert your private key to a `.ppk` file required by PuTTY. Launch `putty.exe`, enter the public IP address of the instance in the **Host Name** field, and set the connection type to SSH.

In the **Category** panel, navigate to **Connection** > **SSH** > **Auth**, and click **Browse** to select your .ppk file, and then click **Open** to connect.

4. The terminal will prompt you to accept the server's public key. Type yes and click **Enter** to complete the connection.

You've now configured a security group, created a key pair, launched an EC2 instance, and connected to it without ever leaving the command line.

Using the AWS Command Line Interface

This section introduces the common features and calling patterns used throughout the AWS Command Line Interface.

Note
The AWS CLI makes API calls to services over HTTPS. Outbound connections on TCP port 443 must be enabled in order to perform calls.

- Getting Help with the AWS Command Line Interface
- Command Structure in the AWS Command Line Interface
- Specifying Parameter Values for the AWS Command Line Interface
- Generate CLI Skeleton and CLI Input JSON Parameters
- Controlling Command Output from the AWS Command Line Interface
- Using Shorthand Syntax with the AWS Command Line Interface
- Using the AWS Command Line Interface's Pagination Options

Getting Help with the AWS Command Line Interface

To get help when using the AWS CLI, you can simply add `help` to the end of a command. For example, the following command lists help for the general AWS CLI options and the available top-level commands.

```
1 $ aws help
```

The following command lists the available subcommands for Amazon EC2.

```
1 $ aws ec2 help
```

The next example lists the detailed help for the EC2 `DescribeInstances` operation, including descriptions of its input parameters, filters, and output. Check the examples section of the help if you are not sure how to phrase a command.

```
1 $ aws ec2 describe-instances help
```

The help for each command is divided into six sections:

Name – the name of the command.

```
1 NAME
2         describe-instances -
```

Description – a description of the API operation that the command invokes, pulled from the API documentation for the command's service.

```
1 DESCRIPTION
2         Describes one or more of your instances.
3
4         If you specify one or more instance IDs, Amazon EC2 returns information
5         for those instances. If you do not specify  instance  IDs,  Amazon  EC2
6         returns  information  for  all  relevant  instances.  If you specify an
7         instance ID that is not valid, an error is returned. If you specify  an
8         instance  that  you  do  not  own,  it  is not included in the returned
9         results.
10 ...
```

Synopsis – list of the command and its options. If an option is shown in square brackets, it is either optional, has a default value, or has an alternative option that can be used instead.

```
1 SYNOPSIS
2            describe-instances
3         [--dry-run | --no-dry-run]
4         [--instance-ids <value>]
5         [--filters <value>]
6         [--cli-input-json <value>]
7         [--starting-token <value>]
8         [--page-size <value>]
9         [--max-items <value>]
10        [--generate-cli-skeleton]
```

`describe-instances` has a default behavior that describes all instances in the current account and region. You can optionally specify a list of `instance-ids` to describe one or more instances. `dry-run` is an optional boolean flag that doesn't take a value. To use a boolean flag, specify either shown value, in this case `--dry-run` or `--no-dry-run`. Likewise, `--generate-cli-skeleton` does not take a value. If there are conditions on an option's use, they should be described in the `OPTIONS` section, or shown in the examples.

Options – description of each of the options shown in the synopsis.

```
 1 OPTIONS
 2        --dry-run | --no-dry-run (boolean)
 3             Checks whether you have the required  permissions  for  the  action,
 4             without actually making the request, and provides an error response.
 5             If you have the required permissions, the error response is  DryRun-
 6             Operation . Otherwise, it is UnauthorizedOperation .
 7
 8        --instance-ids (list)
 9             One or more instance IDs.
10
11             Default: Describes all your instances.
12 ...
```

Examples – examples showing the usage of the command and its options. If no example is available for a command or use case that you need, please request one using the feedback link on this page, or in the AWS CLI command reference on the help page for the command.

```
 1     EXAMPLES
 2     To describe an Amazon EC2 instance
 3
 4     Command:
 5
 6     aws ec2 describe-instances --instance-ids i-5203422c
 7
 8     To describe all instances with the instance type m1.small
 9
10     Command:
11
12     aws ec2 describe-instances --filters "Name=instance-type,Values=m1.small"
13
14     To describe all instances with a Owner tag
15
16     Command:
17
18     aws ec2 describe-instances --filters "Name=tag-key,Values=Owner"
19 ...
```

Output – descriptions of each of the fields and datatypes returned in the response from AWS.

For describe-instances, the output is a list of reservation objects, each of which contains several fields and objects that contain information about the instance(s) associated with it. This information comes from the API documentation for the reservation datatype used by Amazon EC2.

```
 1 OUTPUT
 2        Reservations -> (list)
 3            One or more reservations.
 4
 5            (structure)
 6                Describes a reservation.
 7
 8                ReservationId -> (string)
 9                    The ID of the reservation.
10
11                OwnerId -> (string)
12                    The ID of the AWS account that owns the reservation.
13
```

```
14    RequesterId -> (string)
15        The ID of the requester that launched the instances  on   your
16        behalf (for example, AWS Management Console or Auto Scaling).
17
18    Groups -> (list)
19        One or more security groups.
20
21        (structure)
22            Describes a security group.
23
24            GroupName -> (string)
25                The name of the security group.
26
27            GroupId -> (string)
28                The ID of the security group.
29
30    Instances -> (list)
31        One or more instances.
32
33        (structure)
34            Describes an instance.
35
36            InstanceId -> (string)
37                The ID of the instance.
38
39            ImageId -> (string)
40                The ID of the AMI used to launch the instance.
41
42            State -> (structure)
43                The current state of the instance.
44
45                Code -> (integer)
46                    The  low  byte represents the state. The high byte
47                    is an opaque internal value and should be ignored.
48 ...
```

When the output is rendered into JSON by the AWS CLI, it becomes an array of reservation objects, like this:

```
1  {
2      "Reservations": [
3          {
4              "OwnerId": "012345678901",
5              "ReservationId": "r-4c58f8a0",
6              "Groups": [],
7              "RequesterId": "012345678901",
8              "Instances": [
9                  {
10                     "Monitoring": {
11                         "State": "disabled"
12                     },
13                     "PublicDnsName": "ec2-52-74-16-12.us-west-2.compute.amazonaws.com",
14                     "State": {
15                         "Code": 16,
16                         "Name": "running"
17                     },
```

Each reservation object contains fields describing the reservation and an array of instance objects, each with its own fields (e.g. `PublicDnsName`) and objects (e.g. `State`) that describe it.

Windows Users
Pipe the output of the help command to `more` to view the help file one page at a time. Press the space bar or Page Down to view more of the document, and q to quit.

```
1 > aws ec2 describe-instances help | more
```

AWS CLI Documentation

The AWS Command Line Interface Reference provides the content of all AWS CLI commands' help files, compiled and presented online for easy navigation and viewing on mobile, tablet, and desktop screens.

Help files sometimes contain links that cannot be viewed or followed from the command line view; these are preserved in the online AWS CLI reference.

API Documentation

All subcommands in the AWS CLI correspond to calls made against a service's public API. Each service with a public API, in turn, has a set of API reference documentation that can be found from the service's homepage on the AWS Documentation website.

The content of an API reference varies based on how the API is constructed and which protocol is used. Typically, an API reference will contain detailed information on actions supported by the API, data sent to and from the service, and possible error conditions.

API Documentation Sections

- **Actions** – Detailed information on parameters (including constraints on length or content) and errors specific to an action. Actions correspond to subcommands in the AWS CLI.

- **Data Types** – May contain additional information about object data returned by a subcommand.

- **Common Parameters** – Detailed information about parameters that are used by all of a service's actions.

- **Common Errors** – Detailed information about errors returned by all of a service's actions.

The name and availability of each section may vary depending on the service.

Service-Specific CLIs
Some services have a separate CLI from before a single AWS CLI was created that works with all services. These service-specific CLIs have separate documentation that is linked from the service's documentation page. Documentation for service-specific CLIs does not apply to the AWS CLI.

Command Structure in the AWS Command Line Interface

The AWS CLI uses a multipart structure on the command line. It starts with the base call to `aws`. The next part specifies a top-level command, which often represents an AWS service supported in the AWS CLI. Each AWS service has additional subcommands that specify the operation to perform. The general CLI options, or the specific parameters for an operation, can be specified on the command line in any order. If an exclusive parameter is specified multiple times, then only the *last value* applies.

```
1  $ aws <command> <subcommand> [options and parameters]
```

Parameters can take various types of input values, such as numbers, strings, lists, maps, and JSON structures.

Specifying Parameter Values for the AWS Command Line Interface

Many parameters are simple string or numeric values, such as the key pair name `my-key-pair` in the following example:

```
1 $ aws ec2 create-key-pair --key-name my-key-pair
```

Strings without any space characters may be quoted or unquoted. However, strings that include one or more space characters must be quoted. Use a single quote (') in Linux, macOS, or Unix and Windows PowerShell, or use a double quote (") in the Windows command prompt, as shown in the following examples.

Windows PowerShell, Linux, macOS, or Unix

```
1 $ aws ec2 create-key-pair --key-name 'my key pair'
```

Windows Command Processor

```
1 > aws ec2 create-key-pair --key-name "my key pair"
```

You can also use an equals sign instead of a space. This is typically only necessary if the value of the parameter starts with a hyphen:

```
1 $ aws ec2 delete-key-pair --key-name=-mykey
```

- Common Parameter Types
- Using JSON for Parameters
- Quoting Strings
- Loading Parameters from a File

Common Parameter Types

This section describes some of the common parameter types and the format that the services expect them to conform to. If you are having trouble with the formatting of a parameter for a specific command, check the manual by typing **help** after the command name, for example:

```
1 $ aws ec2 describe-spot-price-history help
```

The help for each subcommand describes its function, options, output, and examples. The options section includes the name and description of each option with the option's parameter type in parentheses.

String – String parameters can contain alphanumeric characters, symbols, and whitespace from the ASCII character set. Strings that contain whitespace must be surrounded by quotes. Use of symbols and whitespace other than the standard space character is not recommended and may cause issues when using the AWS CLI.

Some string parameters can accept binary data from a file. See for an example.

Timestamp – Timestamps are formatted per the ISO 8601 standard. These are sometimes referred to as "DateTime" or "Date" type parameters.

```
1 $ aws ec2 describe-spot-price-history --start-time 2014-10-13T19:00:00Z
```

Acceptable formats include:

- YYYY-MM-DDThh:mm:ss.sssTZD (UTC), e.g., 2014-10-01T20:30:00.000Z
- YYYY-MM-DDThh:mm:ss.sssTZD (with offset), e.g., 2014-10-01T12:30:00.000-08:00
- YYYY-MM-DD, e.g., 2014-10-01
- Unix time in seconds, e.g. 1412195400

List – One or more strings separated by spaces.

```
1  $ aws ec2 describe-spot-price-history --instance-types m1.xlarge m1.medium
```

Boolean – Binary flag that turns an option on or off. For example, `ec2 describe-spot-price-history` has a boolean dry-run parameter that, when specified, validates the command against the service without actually running a query.

```
1  $ aws ec2 describe-spot-price-history --dry-run
```

The output indicates whether the command was well formed or not. This command also includes a no-dry-run version of the parameter that can be used to explicitly indicate that the command should be run normally, although including it is not necessary as this is the default behavior.

Integer – An unsigned whole number.

```
1  $ aws ec2 describe-spot-price-history --max-items 5
```

Blob – Binary object. Blob parameters take a path to a local file that contains binary data. The path should not contain any protocol identifier such as `http://` or `file://`.

The `--body` parameter for `aws s3api put-object` is a blob:

```
1  $  aws s3api put-object --bucket my-bucket --key testimage.png --body /tmp/image.png
```

Map – A sequence of key value pairs specified in JSON or shorthand syntax. The following example reads an item from a DynamoDB table named *my-table* with a map parameter, `--key`. The parameter specifies the primary key named *id* with a number value of *1* in a nested JSON structure.

```
1  $ aws dynamodb get-item --table-name my-table --key '{"id": {"N":"1"}}'
2  {
3      "Item": {
4          "name": {
5              "S": "John"
6          },
7          "id": {
8              "N": "1"
9          }
10     }
11 }
```

The next section covers JSON arguments in more detail.

Using JSON for Parameters

JSON is useful for specifying complex command line parameters. For example, the following command will list all EC2 instances that have an instance type of `m1.small` or `m1.medium` that are also in the `us-west-2c` Availability Zone.

```
1  $ aws ec2 describe-instances --filters "Name=instance-type,Values=t2.micro,m1.medium" "Name=
      availability-zone,Values=us-west-2c"
```

The following example specifies the equivalent list of filters in a JSON array. Square brackets are used to create an array of JSON objects separated by commas. Each object is a comma separated list of key-value pairs ("Name" and "Values" are both keys in this instance).

Note that value to the right of the "Values" key is itself an array. This is required, even if the array contains only one value string.

```
1  [
2    {
3      "Name": "instance-type",
4      "Values": ["t2.micro", "m1.medium"]
5    },
6    {
7      "Name": "availability-zone",
8      "Values": ["us-west-2c"]
9    }
10 ]
```

The outermost brackets, on the other hand, are only required if more than one filter is specified. A single filter version of the above command, formatted in JSON, looks like this:

```
1  $ aws ec2 describe-instances --filters '{"Name": "instance-type", "Values": ["t2.micro", "m1.
     medium"]}'
```

Some operations require data to be formatted as JSON. For example, to pass parameters to the `--block-device-mappings` parameter in the `ec2 run-instances` command, you need to format the block device information as JSON.

This example shows the JSON to specify a single 20 GiB Elastic Block Store device to be mapped at `/dev/sdb` on the launching instance.

```
1  {
2    "DeviceName": "/dev/sdb",
3    "Ebs": {
4      "VolumeSize": 20,
5      "DeleteOnTermination": false,
6      "VolumeType": "standard"
7    }
8  }
```

To attach multiple devices, list the objects in an array like in the next example.

```
1  [
2    {
3      "DeviceName": "/dev/sdb",
4      "Ebs": {
5        "VolumeSize": 20,
6        "DeleteOnTermination": false,
7        "VolumeType": "standard"
8      }
9    },
10   {
11     "DeviceName": "/dev/sdc",
12     "Ebs": {
13       "VolumeSize": 10,
14       "DeleteOnTermination": true,
15       "VolumeType": "standard"
16     }
17   }
18 ]
```

You can either enter the JSON directly on the command line (see Quoting Strings), or save it to a file that is referenced from the command line (see).

When passing in large blocks of data, you might find it easier to save the JSON to a file and reference it from the command line. JSON data in a file is easier to read, edit, and share with others. This technique is described in the next section.

For more information about JSON, see Wikipedia - JSON and RFC4627 - The application/json Media Type for JSON.

Quoting Strings

The way you enter JSON-formatted parameters on the command line differs depending upon your operating system. Linux, macOS, or Unix and Windows PowerShell use the single quote (') to enclose the JSON data structure, as in the following example:

```
1 $ aws ec2 run-instances --image-id ami-05355a6c --block-device-mappings '[{"DeviceName":"/dev/
    sdb","Ebs":{"VolumeSize":20,"DeleteOnTermination":false,"VolumeType":"standard"}}]'
```

The Windows command prompt, on the other hand, uses the double quote (") to enclose the JSON data structure. In addition, a backslash (\) escape character is required for each double quote (") within the JSON data structure itself, as in the following example:

```
1 > aws ec2 run-instances --image-id ami-05355a6c --block-device-mappings "[{\"DeviceName\":\"/dev
    /sdb\",\"Ebs\":{\"VolumeSize\":20,\"DeleteOnTermination\":false,\"VolumeType\":\"standard
    \"}}]"
```

Windows PowerShell requires a single quote (') to enclose the JSON data structure, as well as a backslash (\) to escape each double quote (") within the JSON structure, as in the following example:

```
1 > aws ec2 run-instances --image-id ami-05355a6c --block-device-mappings '[{\"DeviceName\":\"/dev
    /sdb\",\"Ebs\":{\"VolumeSize\":20,\"DeleteOnTermination\":false,\"VolumeType\":\"standard
    \"}}]'
```

If the value of a parameter is itself a JSON document, escape the quotes on the embedded JSON document. For example, the `attribute` parameter for `aws sqs create-queue` can take a `RedrivePolicy` key. The value of `RedrivePolicy` is a JSON document, which must be escaped:

```
1 $ aws sqs create-queue --queue-name my-queue --attributes '{ "RedrivePolicy":"{\"
    deadLetterTargetArn\":\"arn:aws:sqs:us-west-2:0123456789012:deadletter\", \"maxReceiveCount
    \":\"5\"}"}'
```

Loading Parameters from a File

To avoid the need to escape JSON strings at the command line, load the JSON from a file. Load parameters from a local file by providing the path to the file using the `file://` prefix, as in the following examples.

Linux, macOS, or Unix

```
1 // Read from a file in the current directory
2 $ aws ec2 describe-instances --filters file://filter.json
3
4 // Read from a file in /tmp
5 $ aws ec2 describe-instances --filters file:///tmp/filter.json
```

Windows

```
1 // Read from a file in C:\temp
2 > aws ec2 describe-instances --filters file://C:\temp\filter.json
```

The `file://` prefix option supports Unix-style expansions including '~/', './', and '../'. On Windows, the '~/' expression expands to your user directory, stored in the %USERPROFILE% environment variable. For example, on Windows 7 you would typically have a user directory under `C:\Users\User Name\`.

JSON documents that are provided as the value of a parameter key must still be escaped:

```
1 $ aws sqs create-queue --queue-name my-queue --attributes file://attributes.json
```

attributes.json

```
1 {
2   "RedrivePolicy":"{\"deadLetterTargetArn\":\"arn:aws:sqs:us-west-2:0123456789012:deadletter\",
      \"maxReceiveCount\":\"5\"}"
3 }
```

Binary Files

For commands that take binary data as a parameter, specify that the data is binary content by using the `fileb://` prefix. Commands that accept binary data include:

- `aws ec2 run-instances` – `--user-data` parameter.

- `aws s3api put-object` – `--sse-customer-key` parameter.

- `aws kms decrypt` – `--ciphertext-blob` parameter.

The following example generates a binary 256 bit AES key using a Linux command line tool and then provides it to Amazon S3 to encrypt an uploaded file server-side:

```
1 $ dd if=/dev/urandom bs=1 count=32 > sse.key
2 32+0 records in
3 32+0 records out
4 32 bytes (32 B) copied, 0.000164441 s, 195 kB/s
5 $ aws s3api put-object --bucket my-bucket --key test.txt --body test.txt --sse-customer-key
      fileb://sse.key --sse-customer-algorithm AES256
6 {
7    "SSECustomerKeyMD5": "iVg8oWa8sy714+FjtesrJg==",
8    "SSECustomerAlgorithm": "AES256",
9    "ETag": "\"a6118e84b76cf98bf04bbe14b6045c6c\""
10 }
```

Remote Files

The AWS CLI also supports loading parameters from a file hosted on the Internet with an `http://` or `https://` URL. The following example references a file in an Amazon S3 bucket. This allows you to access parameter files from any computer, but requires the file to be stored in a publically accessible location.

```
1 $ aws ec2 run-instances --image-id ami-a13d6891 --block-device-mappings http://my-bucket.s3.
      amazonaws.com/filename.json
```

In the preceding examples, the `filename.json` file contains the following JSON data.

```
1 [
2   {
3     "DeviceName": "/dev/sdb",
4     "Ebs": {
5       "VolumeSize": 20,
```

```
 6        "DeleteOnTermination": false,
 7        "VolumeType": "standard"
 8      }
 9    }
10 ]
```

For another example referencing a file containing more complex JSON-formatted parameters, see .

Generate CLI Skeleton and CLI Input JSON Parameters

Most AWS CLI commands support `--generate-cli-skeleton` and `--cli-input-json` parameters that you can use to store parameters in JSON and read them from a file instead of typing them at the command line.

Generate CLI Skeleton outputs JSON that outlines all of the parameters that can be specified for the operation.

To use --generate-cli-skeleton with aws ec2 run-instances

1. Execute the run-instances command with the `--generate-cli-skeleton` option to view the JSON skeleton.

```
 1 $ aws ec2 run-instances --generate-cli-skeleton
 2 {
 3     "DryRun": true,
 4     "ImageId": "",
 5     "MinCount": 0,
 6     "MaxCount": 0,
 7     "KeyName": "",
 8     "SecurityGroups": [
 9         ""
10     ],
11     "SecurityGroupIds": [
12         ""
13     ],
14     "UserData": "",
15     "InstanceType": "",
16     "Placement": {
17         "AvailabilityZone": "",
18         "GroupName": "",
19         "Tenancy": ""
20     },
21     "KernelId": "",
22     "RamdiskId": "",
23     "BlockDeviceMappings": [
24         {
25             "VirtualName": "",
26             "DeviceName": "",
27             "Ebs": {
28                 "SnapshotId": "",
29                 "VolumeSize": 0,
30                 "DeleteOnTermination": true,
31                 "VolumeType": "",
32                 "Iops": 0,
33                 "Encrypted": true
34             },
35             "NoDevice": ""
36         }
37     ],
38     "Monitoring": {
39         "Enabled": true
40     },
41     "SubnetId": "",
42     "DisableApiTermination": true,
43     "InstanceInitiatedShutdownBehavior": "",
44     "PrivateIpAddress": "",
45     "ClientToken": "",
```

```
46        "AdditionalInfo": "",
47        "NetworkInterfaces": [
48            {
49                 "NetworkInterfaceId": "",
50                 "DeviceIndex": 0,
51                 "SubnetId": "",
52                 "Description": "",
53                 "PrivateIpAddress": "",
54                 "Groups": [
55                     ""
56                 ],
57                 "DeleteOnTermination": true,
58                 "PrivateIpAddresses": [
59                     {
60                         "PrivateIpAddress": "",
61                         "Primary": true
62                     }
63                 ],
64                 "SecondaryPrivateIpAddressCount": 0,
65                 "AssociatePublicIpAddress": true
66            }
67        ],
68        "IamInstanceProfile": {
69            "Arn": "",
70            "Name": ""
71        },
72        "EbsOptimized": true
73  }
```

2. Direct the output to a file to save the skeleton locally:

```
1  $ aws ec2 run-instances --generate-cli-skeleton > ec2runinst.json
```

3. Open the skeleton in a text editor and remove any parameters that you will not use:

```
1  {
2      "DryRun": true,
3      "ImageId": "",
4      "KeyName": "",
5      "SecurityGroups": [
6          ""
7      ],
8      "InstanceType": "",
9      "Monitoring": {
10         "Enabled": true
11     }
12 }
```

Leave the DryRun parameter set to true to use EC2's dry run feature, which lets you test your configuration without creating resources.

4. Fill in the values for the instance type, key name, security group and AMI in your default region. In this example, ami-dfc39aef is a 64-bit Amazon Linux image in the us-west-2 region.

```
1  {
2      "DryRun": true,
3      "ImageId": "ami-dfc39aef",
```

```
4        "KeyName": "mykey",
5        "SecurityGroups": [
6            "my-sg"
7        ],
8        "InstanceType": "t2.micro",
9        "Monitoring": {
10            "Enabled": true
11        }
12   }
```

5. Pass the JSON configuration to the `--cli-input-json` parameter using the `file://` prefix:

```
1  $ aws ec2 run-instances --cli-input-json file://ec2runinst.json
2  A client error (DryRunOperation) occurred when calling the RunInstances operation: Request
     would have succeeded, but DryRun flag is set.
```

The dry run error indicates that the JSON is formed correctly and the parameter values are valid. If any other issues are reported in the output, fix them and repeat the above step until the dry run error is shown.

6. Set the DryRun parameter to false to disable the dry run feature.

```
1  {
2        "DryRun": false,
3        "ImageId": "ami-dfc39aef",
4        "KeyName": "mykey",
5        "SecurityGroups": [
6            "my-sg"
7        ],
8        "InstanceType": "t2.micro",
9        "Monitoring": {
10            "Enabled": true
11        }
12   }
```

7. Run the `run-instances` command again to launch an instance:

```
1  $ aws ec2 run-instances --cli-input-json file://ec2runinst.json
2  {
3        "OwnerId": "123456789012",
4        "ReservationId": "r-d94a2b1",
5        "Groups": [],
6        "Instances": [
7  ...
```

Controlling Command Output from the AWS Command Line Interface

This section describes the different ways that you can control the output from the AWS CLI.

- How to Select the Output Format
- How to Filter the Output with the --query Option
- JSON Output Format
- Text Output Format
- Table Output Format

How to Select the Output Format

The AWS CLI supports three different output formats:

- JSON (json)

- Tab-delimited text (text)

- ASCII-formatted table (table)

As explained in the configuration topic, the output format can be specified in three different ways:

- Using the output option in the configuration file. The following example sets the output to text:

```
1 [default]
2 output=text
```

- Using the AWS_DEFAULT_OUTPUT environment variable. For example:

```
1 $ export AWS_DEFAULT_OUTPUT="table"
```

- Using the --output option on the command line. For example:

```
1 $ aws swf list-domains --registration-status REGISTERED --output text
```

Note
If the output format is specified in multiple ways, the usual AWS CLI precedence rules apply. For example, using the AWS_DEFAULT_OUTPUT environment variable overrides any value set in the config file with output, and a value passed to an AWS CLI command with --output overrides any value set in the environment or in the config file.

JSON is best for handling the output programmatically via various languages or jq (a command-line JSON processor). The table format is easy for humans to read, and text format works well with traditional Unix text processing tools, such as **sed**, **grep**, and **awk**, as well as Windows PowerShell scripts.

How to Filter the Output with the --query Option

The AWS CLI provides built-in output filtering capabilities with the --query option. To demonstrate how it works, we'll first start with the default JSON output below, which describes two EBS (Elastic Block Storage) volumes attached to separate EC2 instances.

```
1 $ aws ec2 describe-volumes
2 {
3     "Volumes": [
4         {
5             "AvailabilityZone": "us-west-2a",
```

```
 6          "Attachments": [
 7              {
 8                  "AttachTime": "2013-09-17T00:55:03.000Z",
 9                  "InstanceId": "i-a071c394",
10                  "VolumeId": "vol-e11a5288",
11                  "State": "attached",
12                  "DeleteOnTermination": true,
13                  "Device": "/dev/sda1"
14              }
15          ],
16          "VolumeType": "standard",
17          "VolumeId": "vol-e11a5288",
18          "State": "in-use",
19          "SnapshotId": "snap-f23ec1c8",
20          "CreateTime": "2013-09-17T00:55:03.000Z",
21          "Size": 30
22      },
23      {
24          "AvailabilityZone": "us-west-2a",
25          "Attachments": [
26              {
27                  "AttachTime": "2013-09-18T20:26:16.000Z",
28                  "InstanceId": "i-4b41a37c",
29                  "VolumeId": "vol-2e410a47",
30                  "State": "attached",
31                  "DeleteOnTermination": true,
32                  "Device": "/dev/sda1"
33              }
34          ],
35          "VolumeType": "standard",
36          "VolumeId": "vol-2e410a47",
37          "State": "in-use",
38          "SnapshotId": "snap-708e8348",
39          "CreateTime": "2013-09-18T20:26:15.000Z",
40          "Size": 8
41      }
42  ]
43 }
```

First, we can display only the first volume from the Volumes list with the following command.

```
 1 $ aws ec2 describe-volumes --query 'Volumes[0]'
 2 {
 3     "AvailabilityZone": "us-west-2a",
 4     "Attachments": [
 5         {
 6             "AttachTime": "2013-09-17T00:55:03.000Z",
 7             "InstanceId": "i-a071c394",
 8             "VolumeId": "vol-e11a5288",
 9             "State": "attached",
10             "DeleteOnTermination": true,
11             "Device": "/dev/sda1"
12         }
13     ],
14     "VolumeType": "standard",
```

```
15      "VolumeId": "vol-e11a5288",
16      "State": "in-use",
17      "SnapshotId": "snap-f23ec1c8",
18      "CreateTime": "2013-09-17T00:55:03.000Z",
19      "Size": 30
20  }
```

Now, we use the wildcard notation [*] to iterate over the entire list and also filter out three elements: VolumeId, AvailabilityZone, and Size. Note that the dictionary notation requires that you provide an alias for each key, like this: {Alias1:Key1,Alias2:Key2}. A dictionary is inherently *unordered*, so the ordering of the key-aliases within a structure may not be consistent in some cases.

```
1  $ aws ec2 describe-volumes --query 'Volumes[*].{ID:VolumeId,AZ:AvailabilityZone,Size:Size}'
2  [
3      {
4          "AZ": "us-west-2a",
5          "ID": "vol-e11a5288",
6          "Size": 30
7      },
8      {
9          "AZ": "us-west-2a",
10         "ID": "vol-2e410a47",
11         "Size": 8
12     }
13 ]
```

In the dictionary notation, you can also use chained keys such as key1.key2[0].key3 to filter elements deeply nested within the structure. The example below demonstrates this with the Attachments[0].InstanceId key, aliased to simply InstanceId.

```
1  $ aws ec2 describe-volumes --query 'Volumes[*].{ID:VolumeId,InstanceId:Attachments[0].InstanceId
      ,AZ:AvailabilityZone,Size:Size}'
2  [
3      {
4          "InstanceId": "i-a071c394",
5          "AZ": "us-west-2a",
6          "ID": "vol-e11a5288",
7          "Size": 30
8      },
9      {
10         "InstanceId": "i-4b41a37c",
11         "AZ": "us-west-2a",
12         "ID": "vol-2e410a47",
13         "Size": 8
14     }
15 ]
```

You can also filter multiple elements with the list notation: [key1, key2]. This will format all filtered attributes into a single *ordered* list per object, regardless of type.

```
1  $ aws ec2 describe-volumes --query 'Volumes[*].[VolumeId, Attachments[0].InstanceId,
      AvailabilityZone, Size]'
2  [
3      [
4          "vol-e11a5288",
5          "i-a071c394",
```

```
6          "us-west-2a",
7          30
8      ],
9      [
10         "vol-2e410a47",
11         "i-4b41a37c",
12         "us-west-2a",
13         8
14     ]
15 ]
```

To filter results by the value of a specific field, use the JMESPath "?" operator. The following example query outputs only volumes in the us-west-2a availability zone:

```
1 $ aws ec2 describe-volumes --query 'Volumes[?AvailabilityZone==`us-west-2a`]'
```

Note

When specifying a literal value such as "us-west-2" above in a JMESPath query expression, you must surround the value in backticks (') in order for it to be read properly.

Combined with the three output formats that will be explained in more detail in the following sections, the --query option is a powerful tool you can use to customize the content and style of outputs. For more examples and the full spec of JMESPath, the underlying JSON-processing library, visit http://jmespath.org/specification.html.

JSON Output Format

JSON is the default output format of the AWS CLI. Most languages can easily decode JSON strings using built-in functions or with publicly available libraries. As shown in the previous topic along with output examples, the --query option provides powerful ways to filter and format the AWS CLI's JSON formatted output. If you need more advanced features that may not be possible with --query, you can check out jq, a command line JSON processor. You can download it and find the official tutorial at: http://stedolan.github.io/jq/.

Text Output Format

The *text* format organizes the AWS CLI's output into tab-delimited lines. It works well with traditional Unix text tools such as grep, sed, and awk, as well as Windows PowerShell.

The text output format follows the basic structure shown below. The columns are sorted alphabetically by the corresponding key names of the underlying JSON object.

```
1 IDENTIFIER  sorted-column1 sorted-column2
2 IDENTIFIER2 sorted-column1 sorted-column2
```

The following is an example of a text output.

```
1 $ aws ec2 describe-volumes --output text
2 VOLUMES us-west-2a       2013-09-17T00:55:03.000Z        30      snap-f23ec1c8   in-use  vol-
     e11a5288    standard
3 ATTACHMENTS     2013-09-17T00:55:03.000Z        True    /dev/sda1       i-a071c394      attached
         vol-e11a5288
4 VOLUMES us-west-2a       2013-09-18T20:26:15.000Z        8       snap-708e8348   in-use  vol-2
     e410a47     standard
5 ATTACHMENTS     2013-09-18T20:26:16.000Z        True    /dev/sda1       i-4b41a37c      attached
         vol-2e410a47
```

We strongly recommend that the text output be used along with the --query option to ensure consistent behavior. This is because the text format alphabetically orders output columns, and similar resources may not always have the same collection of keys. For example, a JSON representation of a Linux EC2 instance may have elements that are not present in the JSON representation of a Windows instance, or vice versa. Also, resources may have key-value elements added or removed in future updates, altering the column ordering. This is where --query augments the functionality of the text output to enable complete control over the output format. In the example below, the command pre-selects which elements to display and defines the ordering of the columns with the list notation [key1, key2, ...]. This gives users full confidence that the correct key values will always be displayed in the expected column. Finally, notice how the AWS CLI outputs 'None' as values for keys that don't exist.

```
1 $ aws ec2 describe-volumes --query 'Volumes[*].[VolumeId, Attachments[0].InstanceId,
      AvailabilityZone, Size, FakeKey]' --output text
2 vol-e11a5288    i-a071c394      us-west-2a      30      None
3 vol-2e410a47    i-4b41a37c      us-west-2a      8       None
```

Below is an example of how **grep** and **awk** can be used along with a text output from `aws ec2 describe-instances` command. The first command displays the Availability Zone, state, and instance ID of each instance in text output. The second command outputs only the instance IDs of all running instances in the us-west-2a Availability Zone.

```
1 $ aws ec2 describe-instances --query 'Reservations[*].Instances[*].[Placement.AvailabilityZone,
      State.Name, InstanceId]' --output text
2 us-west-2a      running i-4b41a37c
3 us-west-2a      stopped i-a071c394
4 us-west-2b      stopped i-97a217a0
5 us-west-2a      running i-3045b007
6 us-west-2a      running i-6fc67758
7
8 $ aws ec2 describe-instances --query 'Reservations[*].Instances[*].[Placement.AvailabilityZone,
      State.Name, InstanceId]' --output text | grep us-west-2a | grep running | awk '{print $3}'
9 i-4b41a37c
10 i-3045b007
11 i-6fc67758
```

The next command shows a similar example for all stopped instances and takes it one step further to automate changing instance types for each stopped instance.

```
1 $ aws ec2 describe-instances --query 'Reservations[*].Instances[*].[State.Name, InstanceId]' --
      output text |
2 > grep stopped |
3 > awk '{print $2}' |
4 > while read line;
5 > do aws ec2 modify-instance-attribute --instance-id $line --instance-type '{"Value": "m1.medium
      "}';
6 > done
```

The text output is useful in Windows PowerShell as well. Because AWS CLI's text output is tab-delimited, it is easily split into an array in PowerShell using the "tdelimiter\. The following command displays the value of the third column \(InstanceId') if the first column ('AvailabilityZone') matches 'us-west-2a'.

```
1 > aws ec2 describe-instances --query 'Reservations[*].Instances[*].[Placement.AvailabilityZone,
      State.Name, InstanceId]' --output text |
2 %{if ($_.split("`t")[0] -match "us-west-2a") { $_.split("`t")[2]; } }
3 i-4b41a37c
4 i-a071c394
5 i-3045b007
```

```
6 i-6fc67758
```

Table Output Format

The `table` format produces human-readable representations of AWS CLI output. Here is an example:

```
1 $ aws ec2 describe-volumes --output table
2 ------------------------------------------------------------------------------------------------------
3 |                                              DescribeVolumes                                        |
   |                                                    |
4 +----------------------------------------------------------------------------------------------------
5 ||                                              Volumes                                              |
   |                                                    ||
6 |+-----------------+----------------------------+-------+----------------+---------+----------------+
7 || AvailabilityZone |         CreateTime         | Size | SnapshotId     | State   | VolumeId
          | VolumeType    ||
8 |+-----------------+----------------------------+-------+----------------+---------+----------------+
9 || us-west-2a       | 2013-09-17T00:55:03.000Z |  30  | snap-f23ec1c8 | in-use | vol-
   e11a5288    | standard      ||
10 |+-----------------+----------------------------+-------+----------------+---------+----------------+
11 |||                                            Attachments
   |||
12 ||+-----------------+----------------------------+---------------+--------------+-----------------+---
13 |||        AttachTime        | DeleteOnTermination  | Device  | InstanceId  |  State
          | VolumeId      |||
14 ||+-----------------+----------------------------+---------------+--------------+-----------------+---
15 ||| 2013-09-17T00:55:03.000Z | True                 | /dev/sda1 | i-a071c394 | attached
   | vol-e11a5288  |||
16 ||+-----------------+----------------------------+---------------+--------------+-----------------+---
17 ||                                              Volumes
   ||
18 |+-----------------+----------------------------+-------+----------------+---------+----------------+
19 || AvailabilityZone |         CreateTime         | Size | SnapshotId     | State   | VolumeId
          | VolumeType    ||
20 |+-----------------+----------------------------+-------+----------------+---------+----------------+
21 || us-west-2a       | 2013-09-18T20:26:15.000Z |  8   | snap-708e8348 | in-use | vol-2
   e410a47    | standard      ||
22 |+-----------------+----------------------------+-------+----------------+---------+----------------+
23 |||                                            Attachments
   |||
24 ||+-----------------+----------------------------+---------------+--------------+-----------------+---
```

```
25 |||          AttachTime        | DeleteOnTermination  |  Device   | InstanceId    |   State
         |  VolumeId     |||
26 ||+------------------------+----------------------+-----------+---------------+------------+---

27 |||  2013-09-18T20:26:16.000Z |  True                |  /dev/sda1 |  i-4b41a37c  |   attached
         |  vol-2e410a47  |||
28 ||+------------------------+----------------------+-----------+---------------+------------+---
```

The --query option can be used with the table format to display a set of elements pre-selected from the raw output. Note the output differences in dictionary and list notations: column names are alphabetically ordered in the first example, and unnamed columns are ordered as defined by the user in the second example.

```
1 $ aws ec2 describe-volumes --query 'Volumes[*].{ID:VolumeId,InstanceId:Attachments[0].InstanceId
     ,AZ:AvailabilityZone,Size:Size}' --output table
2 -------------------------------------------------------
3 |                   DescribeVolumes                   |
4 +------------+----------------+--------------+-------+
5 |     AZ     |      ID        |  InstanceId  | Size  |
6 +------------+----------------+--------------+-------+
7 | us-west-2a|  vol-e11a5288  |  i-a071c394  |  30   |
8 | us-west-2a|  vol-2e410a47  |  i-4b41a37c  |  8    |
9 +------------+----------------+--------------+-------+
10
11 $ aws ec2 describe-volumes --query 'Volumes[*].[VolumeId,Attachments[0].InstanceId,
     AvailabilityZone,Size]' --output table
12 -------------------------------------------------------
13 |                   DescribeVolumes                   |
14 +--------------+--------------+--------------+-----+
15 | vol-e11a5288|  i-a071c394  |  us-west-2a  |  30 |
16 | vol-2e410a47|  i-4b41a37c  |  us-west-2a  |  8  |
17 +--------------+--------------+--------------+-----+
```

Using Shorthand Syntax with the AWS Command Line Interface

While the AWS Command Line Interface can take nonscalar option parameters in JSON format, it can be tedious to type large JSON lists or structures on the command line. To address this issue, the AWS CLI supports a shorthand syntax that allows simpler representation of your option parameters than using the full JSON format.

Structure Parameters

The shorthand syntax in the AWS CLI makes it easier for users to input parameters that are flat (non-nested structures). The format is a comma separate list of key value pairs:

Linux, macOS, or Unix

```
1  --option key1=value1,key2=value2,key3=value3
```

Windows PowerShell

```
1  --option "key1=value1,key2=value2,key3=value3"
```

This is equivalent to the following example formatted in JSON:

```
1  --option '{"key1":"value1","key2":"value2","key3":"value3"}'
```

There must be no whitespace between each comma-separated key/value pair. Here is an example of the DynamoDB `update-table` command with the `--provisioned-throughput` option specified in shorthand.

```
1  $ aws dynamodb update-table --provisioned-throughput ReadCapacityUnits=15,WriteCapacityUnits=10
      --table-name MyDDBTable
```

This is equivalent to the following example formatted in JSON:

```
1  $ aws dynamodb update-table --provisioned-throughput '{"ReadCapacityUnits":15,"
      WriteCapacityUnits":10}' --table-name MyDDBTable
```

List Parameters

Input parameters in a list form can be specified in two ways: JSON and shorthand. The AWS CLI's shorthand syntax is designed to make it easier to pass in lists with number, string, or non-nested structures. The basic format is shown here, where values in the list are separated by a single space.

```
1  --option value1 value2 value3
```

This is equivalent to the following example formatted in JSON.

```
1  --option '[value1,value2,value3]'
```

As previously mentioned, you can specify a list of numbers, a list of strings, or a list of non-nested structures in shorthand. The following is an example of the **stop-instances** command for Amazon EC2, where the input parameter (list of strings) for the `--instance-ids` option is specified in shorthand.

```
1  $ aws ec2 stop-instances --instance-ids i-1486157a i-1286157c i-ec3a7e87
```

This is equivalent to the following example formatted in JSON.

```
1  $ aws ec2 stop-instances --instance-ids '["i-1486157a","i-1286157c","i-ec3a7e87"]'
```

Next is an example of the Amazon EC2 **create-tags** command, which takes a list of non-nested structures for the `--tags` option. The `--resources` option specifies the ID of the instance to be tagged.

```
1 $ aws ec2 create-tags --resources i-1286157c --tags Key=My1stTag,Value=Value1 Key=My2ndTag,Value
    =Value2 Key=My3rdTag,Value=Value3
```

This is equivalent to the following example formatted in JSON. The JSON parameter is written in multiple lines for readability.

```
1 $ aws ec2 create-tags --resources i-1286157c --tags '[
2   {"Key": "My1stTag", "Value": "Value1"},
3   {"Key": "My2ndTag", "Value": "Value2"},
4   {"Key": "My3rdTag", "Value": "Value3"}
5 ]'
```

Using the AWS Command Line Interface's Pagination Options

For commands that can return a large list of items, the AWS CLI adds three options that you can use to modify the pagination behavior of the CLI when it calls a service's API to populate the list.

By default, the CLI uses a page size of 1000 and retrieves all available items. For example, if you run `aws s3api list-objects` on an Amazon S3 bucket containing 3500 objects, the CLI makes four calls to Amazon S3, handling the service specific pagination logic in the background.

If you see issues when running list commands on a large number of resources, the default page size may be too high, causing calls to AWS services to time out. You can use the `--page-size` option to specify a smaller page size to solve this issue. The CLI will still retrieve the full list, but will perform a larger number of calls in the background, retrieving a smaller number of items with each call:

```
1 $ aws s3api list-objects --bucket my-bucket --page-size 100
2 {
3     "Contents": [
4 ...
```

To retrieve fewer items, use the `--max-items` option. The CLI will handle pagination in the same way, but will only print out the number of items that you specify:

```
1 $ aws s3api list-objects --bucket my-bucket --max-items 100
2 {
3     "NextToken": "eyJNYXJrZXIiOiBudWxsLCAiYm90b190cnVuY2F0ZV9hbW91bnQiOiAxfQ==",
4     "Contents": [
5 ...
```

If the number of items output (`--max-items`) is fewer than the total number of items, the output includes a `NextToken` that you can pass in a subsequent command to retrieve the next set of items:

```
1 $ aws s3api list-objects --bucket my-bucket --max-items 100 --starting-token
      eyJNYXJrZXIiOiBudWxsLCAiYm90b190cnVuY2F0ZV9hbW91bnQiOiAxfQ==
2 {
3     "NextToken": "eyJNYXJrZXIiOiBudWxsLCAiYm90b190cnVuY2F0ZV9hbW91bnQiOiAyfQ==",
4     "Contents": [
5 ...
```

A service may not return items in the same order each time you call. If you specify a next token in the middle of a page, you may see different results that you expect. To prevent this, use the same number for `--page-size` and `--max-items`, to sync the CLI's pagination with the service's. You can also retrieve the whole list and perform any necessary parsing operations locally.

Working with Amazon Web Services

This section provides examples of using the AWS Command Line Interface to access AWS services. These examples are intended to demonstrate how to use the AWS CLI to perform administrative tasks.

For a complete reference to all of the available commands for each service, see the AWS Command Line Interface Reference or use the built-in command line help. For more information, see .

- Using Amazon DynamoDB with the AWS Command Line Interface
- Using Amazon EC2 through the AWS Command Line Interface
- Using Amazon Glacier with the AWS Command Line Interface
- AWS Identity and Access Management from the AWS Command Line Interface
- Using Amazon S3 with the AWS Command Line Interface
- Using the AWS Command Line Interface with Amazon SNS
- Using Amazon Simple Workflow Service with the AWS Command Line Interface

Using Amazon DynamoDB with the AWS Command Line Interface

The AWS Command Line Interface (AWS CLI) provides support for Amazon DynamoDB. You can use the AWS CLI for ad hoc operations, such as creating a table. You can also use it to embed DynamoDB operations within utility scripts.

The command line format consists of an Amazon DynamoDB API name, followed by the parameters for that API. The AWS CLI supports a shorthand syntax for the parameter values, as well as JSON.

For example, the following command will create a table named `MusicCollection`.

Note

For readability, long commands in this section are broken into separate lines. The backslash character lets you copy and paste (or type) multiple lines into a Linux terminal. If you are using a shell that does not use backslash to escape characters, replace the backslash with another escape character, or remove the backslashes and put the entire command on a single line.

```
1 $ aws dynamodb create-table \
2     --table-name MusicCollection \
3     --attribute-definitions \
4         AttributeName=Artist,AttributeType=S AttributeName=SongTitle,AttributeType=S \
5     --key-schema AttributeName=Artist,KeyType=HASH AttributeName=SongTitle,KeyType=RANGE \
6     --provisioned-throughput ReadCapacityUnits=1,WriteCapacityUnits=1
```

The following commands will add new items to the table. These example use a combination of shorthand syntax and JSON.

```
1 $ aws dynamodb put-item \
2     --table-name MusicCollection \
3     --item '{
4         "Artist": {"S": "No One You Know"},
5         "SongTitle": {"S": "Call Me Today"} ,
6         "AlbumTitle": {"S": "Somewhat Famous"} }' \
7     --return-consumed-capacity TOTAL
8 {
9     "ConsumedCapacity": {
10         "CapacityUnits": 1.0,
11         "TableName": "MusicCollection"
12     }
13 }
14 $ aws dynamodb put-item \
15     --table-name MusicCollection \
16     --item '{
17         "Artist": {"S": "Acme Band"},
18         "SongTitle": {"S": "Happy Day"} ,
19         "AlbumTitle": {"S": "Songs About Life"} }' \
20     --return-consumed-capacity TOTAL
21 {
22     "ConsumedCapacity": {
23         "CapacityUnits": 1.0,
24         "TableName": "MusicCollection"
25     }
26 }
```

On the command line, it can be difficult to compose valid JSON; however, the AWS CLI can read JSON files. For example, consider the following JSON snippet, which is stored in a file named `expression-attributes.json`:

Example expression-attributes.json

```
1 {
2   ":v1": {"S": "No One You Know"},
3   ":v2": {"S": "Call Me Today"}
4 }
```

You can now issue a `Query` request using the AWS CLI. In this example, the contents of the `expression-attributes.json` file are used for the `--expression-attribute-values` parameter:

```
1 $ aws dynamodb query --table-name MusicCollection \
2     --key-condition-expression "Artist = :v1 AND SongTitle = :v2" \
3     --expression-attribute-values file://expression-attributes.json
4 {
5     "Count": 1,
6     "Items": [
7         {
8             "AlbumTitle": {
9                 "S": "Somewhat Famous"
10            },
11            "SongTitle": {
12                "S": "Call Me Today"
13            },
14            "Artist": {
15                "S": "No One You Know"
16            }
17        }
18    ],
19    "ScannedCount": 1,
20    "ConsumedCapacity": null
21 }
```

For more documentation on using the AWS CLI with DynamoDB, go to http://docs.aws.amazon.com/cli/latest/reference/dynamodb/index.html.

In addition to DynamoDB, you can use the AWS CLI with DynamoDB Local. DynamoDB Local is a small client-side database and server that mimics the DynamoDB service. DynamoDB Local enables you to write applications that use the DynamoDB API, without actually manipulating any tables or data in DynamoDB. Instead, all of the API actions are rerouted to DynamoDB Local. When your application creates a table or modifies data, those changes are written to a local database. This lets you save on provisioned throughput, data storage, and data transfer fees.

For more information about DynamoDB Local and how to use it with the AWS CLI, see the following sections of the Amazon DynamoDB Developer Guide:

- DynamoDB Local
- Using the AWS CLI with DynamoDB Local

Using Amazon EC2 through the AWS Command Line Interface

You can access the features of Amazon EC2 using the AWS CLI. To list the AWS CLI commands for Amazon EC2, use the following command.

```
1 $ aws ec2 help
```

Before you run any commands, set your default credentials. For more information, see Configuring the AWS CLI.

For examples of common tasks for Amazon EC2, see the following topics.

- Using Key Pairs
- Using Security Groups
- Using Amazon EC2 Instances

Using Key Pairs

You can use the AWS CLI to create, display, and delete your key pairs. You must specify a key pair when you launch and connect to an Amazon EC2 instance.

Note

Before you try the example commands, set your default credentials.

- Creating a Key Pair
- Displaying Your Key Pair
- Deleting Your Key Pair

Creating a Key Pair

To create a key pair named `MyKeyPair`, use the create-key-pair command, and use the `--query` option and the `--output text` option to pipe your private key directly into a file.

```
1 $ aws ec2 create-key-pair --key-name MyKeyPair --query 'KeyMaterial' --output text > MyKeyPair.
    pem
```

Note that for Windows PowerShell, the `>` `file` redirection defaults to UTF-8 encoding, which cannot be used with some SSH clients. So, you must explicitly specify ASCII encoding in the `out-file` command.

```
1 > aws ec2 create-key-pair --key-name MyKeyPair --query 'KeyMaterial' --output text | out-file -
    encoding ascii -filepath MyKeyPair.pem
```

The resulting `MyKeyPair.pem` file looks like this:

```
1  -----BEGIN RSA PRIVATE KEY-----
2  EXAMPLEKEYKCAQEAy7WZhaDsrA1W3mRlQtvhwyORRX8gnxgDAfRt/gx42kWXsT4rXE/b5CpSgie/
3  vBoU7jLxx92pNHoFnByP+Dc21eyyz6CvjTmWAOJwfWiW5/akH7iO5dSrvC7dQkW2duV5QuUdEOQW
4  Z/aNxMniGQE6XAgfwlnXVBwrerrQo+ZWQeqiUwwMkuEbLeJFLhMCvYURpUMSC1oehm449ilx9X1F
5  G50TCFeOzfl8dqqCP6GzbPaIjiU19xX/azOR9V+tpUOzEL+wmXnZt3/nHPQ5xvD20JH67km6SuPW
6  oPzev/D8V+x4+bHthfSjR9Y7DvQFjfBVwHXigBdtZcU2/wei8D/HYwIDAQABAoIBAGZ1kaEvnrqu
7  /uler7vgIn5m7lN5LKw4hJLAIW6tUT/fzvtcHKOSkbQCQXuriHmQ2MQyJX/Okn2NfjLV/ufGxbL1
8  mb5qwMGUnEpJaZD6QSSs3kICLwWUYUiGfcOuiSbmJoap/GTLUOW5Mfcv36PaBUNy5p53V6G7hXb2
9  bahyWyJNfjLe4M86yd2YK3V2CmK+X/BOsShnJ36+hjrXPPWmV3N9zEmCdJjA+K15DYmhm/tJWSD9
10 81oGk9TopEp7CkIfatEATyyZiVqoRq6k64iuM9JkA3OzdXzMQexXVJ1TLZVEHOE7bhlY9d8O1ozR
11 oQs/FiZNAx2iijCWyvOlpjE73+kCgYEA9mZtyhkHkFDpwrSM1APaL8oNAbbjwEy7Z5Mqfql+lIp1
12 YkriLODbLXlvRAH+yHPRit2hHOjtUNZh4Axv+cpg09qbUI3+43eEy24B7G/Uh+GTfbjsXsOxQx/x
13 p9otyVwc7hsQ5TA5PZb+mvkJ5OBEKzet9XcKwONBYELGhnEPe7cCgYEAO6Vgov6YHleHui9kHuws
14 ayav0elc5zkxjF9nfHFJRry21R1trw2Vdpn+9g481URrpzWVOEihvm+xTtmaZlSp//lkq75XDwnU
15 WA8gkn6O3QE3fq2yN98BURsAKdJfJ5RL1HvGQvTe1OHLYYXpJnEkHv+Unl2ajLivWUt5pbBrKbUC
16 gYBjbO+OZk0sCcpZ29sbzjYjpIddErySIyRX5gV2uNQwAjLdp9PfN295yQ+BxMBXiIycWVQiwObH
17 oMo7yykABY7Ozd5wQewBQ4AdSlWSX4nGDtsiFxWiI5sKuAAeOCbTosy1s8w8fxoJ5Tz1sdoxNeGs
18 Arq6Wv/G16zQuAE9zK9vvwKBgF+O9VI/1wJBirsDGz9whVWfFPrTkJNvJZzYt69qezxlsjgFKshy
19 WBhd4xHZtmCqpBPlAymEjr/TOlbxyARmXMnIOWIAnNXMGB4KGSyl1mzSVAoQ+fqR+cJ3dOdyPl1j
20 jjbOEd/NY8frlNDxAVHE8BSkdsx2f6ELEyBKJSRr9snRAoGAMrTwYneXzvTskF/S5Fyu0iOegLDa
21 NWUH38v/nDCgEpIXD5Hn3qAEcju1IjmbwlvtW+nY2jVhv7UGd8MjwUTNGItdb6nsYqM2asrnF3qS
22 VRkAKKKYeGjkpUfVTrWOYFjXkfcrR/V+QFL5OndHAKJXjW7a4ejJLncTzmZSpYzwApc=
23 -----END RSA PRIVATE KEY-----
```

Your private key is not stored in AWS and can only be retrieved when it is created.

If you're using an SSH client on a Linux computer to connect to your instance, use the following command to set the permissions of your private key file so that only you can read it.

71

```
1 $ chmod 400 MyKeyPair.pem
```

Displaying Your Key Pair

A fingerprint is generated from your key pair, and you can use it to verify that the private key that you have on your local machine matches the public key that's stored in AWS. The fingerprint is an SHA1 hash taken from a DER encoded copy of the private key. This value is stored in AWS and can be viewed in the EC2 management console or by calling `aws ec2 describe-key-pairs`. For example, you can view the fingerprint for `MyKeyPair` by using the following command:

```
1 $ aws ec2 describe-key-pairs --key-name MyKeyPair
2 {
3     "KeyPairs": [
4         {
5             "KeyName": "MyKeyPair",
6             "KeyFingerprint": "1f:51:ae:28:bf:89:e9:d8:1f:25:5d:37:2d:7d:b8:ca:9f:f5:f1:6f"
7         }
8     ]
9 }
```

For more information on keys and fingerprints, see the Amazon EC2 Key Pairs page in the Amazon EC2 User Guide.

Deleting Your Key Pair

To delete `MyKeyPair`, use the delete-key-pair command as follows:

```
1 $ aws ec2 delete-key-pair --key-name MyKeyPair
```

Using Security Groups

You create a security group for use in either EC2-Classic or EC2-VPC. For more information about EC2-Classic and EC2-VPC, see Supported Platforms in the *Amazon EC2 User Guide for Linux Instances*.

You can use the AWS CLI to create, add rules to, and delete your security groups.

Note
Before you try the example commands, set your default credentials.

- Creating a Security Group
- Adding Rules to Your Security Group
- Deleting Your Security Group

Creating a Security Group

To create a security group named my-sg, use the create-security-group command.

EC2-VPC

The following command creates a security group named my-sg for the specified VPC:

```
1 $ aws ec2 create-security-group --group-name my-sg --description "My security group" --vpc-id
    vpc-1a2b3c4d
2 {
3     "GroupId": "sg-903004f8"
4 }
```

To view the initial information for my-sg, use the describe-security-groups command as follows. Note that you can't reference a security group for EC2-VPC by name.

```
1  $ aws ec2 describe-security-groups --group-ids sg-903004f8
2  {
3      "SecurityGroups": [
4          {
5              "IpPermissionsEgress": [
6                  {
7                      "IpProtocol": "-1",
8                      "IpRanges": [
9                          {
10                             "CidrIp": "0.0.0.0/0"
11                         }
12                     ],
13                     "UserIdGroupPairs": []
14                 }
15             ],
16             "Description": "My security group"
17             "IpPermissions": [],
18             "GroupName": "my-sg",
19             "VpcId": "vpc-1a2b3c4d",
20             "OwnerId": "123456789012",
21             "GroupId": "sg-903004f8"
22         }
23     ]
24 }
```

EC2-Classic

The following command creates a security group for EC2-Classic:

```
1 $ aws ec2 create-security-group --group-name my-sg --description "My security group"
2 {
3     "GroupId": "sg-903004f8"
4 }
```

To view the initial information for my-sg, use the describe-security-groups command as follows:

```
1 $ aws ec2 describe-security-groups --group-names my-sg
2 {
3     "SecurityGroups": [
4         {
5             "IpPermissionsEgress": [],
6             "Description": "My security group"
7             "IpPermissions": [],
8             "GroupName": "my-sg",
9             "OwnerId": "123456789012",
10            "GroupId": "sg-903004f8"
11        }
12    ]
13 }
```

Adding Rules to Your Security Group

If you're launching a Windows instance, you must add a rule to allow inbound traffic on TCP port 3389 (RDP). If you're launching a Linux instance, you must add a rule to allow inbound traffic on TCP port 22 (SSH). Use the authorize-security-group-ingress command to add a rule to your security group. One of the required parameters of this command is the public IP address of your computer, in CIDR notation.

Note
You can get the public IP address of your local computer using a service. For example, we provide the following service: http://checkip.amazonaws.com/. To locate another service that provides your IP address, use the search phrase "what is my IP address". If you are connecting through an ISP or from behind your firewall without a static IP address, you need to find out the range of IP addresses used by client computers.

EC2-VPC

The following command adds a rule for RDP to the security group with the ID sg-903004f8:

```
1 $ aws ec2 authorize-security-group-ingress --group-id sg-903004f8 --protocol tcp --port 3389 --
    cidr 203.0.113.0/24
```

The following command adds a rule for SSH to the security group with the ID sg-903004f8:

```
1 $ aws ec2 authorize-security-group-ingress --group-id sg-903004f8 --protocol tcp --port 22 --
    cidr 203.0.113.0/24
```

To view the changes to my-sg, use the describe-security-groups command as follows:

```
1 $ aws ec2 describe-security-groups --group-ids sg-903004f8
2 {
3     "SecurityGroups": [
4         {
```

```
 5          "IpPermissionsEgress": [
 6              {
 7                  "IpProtocol": "-1",
 8                  "IpRanges": [
 9                      {
10                          "CidrIp": "0.0.0.0/0"
11                      }
12                  ],
13                  "UserIdGroupPairs": []
14              }
15          ],
16          "Description": "My security group"
17          "IpPermissions": [
18              {
19                  "ToPort": 22,
20                  "IpProtocol": "tcp",
21                  "IpRanges": [
22                      {
23                          "CidrIp": "203.0.113.0/24"
24                      }
25                  ]
26                  "UserIdGroupPairs": [],
27                  "FromPort": 22
28              }
29          ],
30          "GroupName": "my-sg",
31          "OwnerId": "123456789012",
32          "GroupId": "sg-903004f8"
33      }
34   ]
35 }
```

EC2-Classic

The following command adds a rule for RDP to the security group `my-sg`:

```
1 $ aws ec2 authorize-security-group-ingress --group-name my-sg --protocol tcp --port 3389 --cidr
    203.0.113.0/24
```

The following command adds a rule for SSH to the security group for `my-sg`:

```
1 $ aws ec2 authorize-security-group-ingress --group-name my-sg --protocol tcp --port 22 --cidr
    203.0.113.0/24
```

To view the changes to `my-sg`, use the describe-security-groups command as follows:

```
1 $ aws ec2 describe-security-groups --group-names my-sg
2 {
3     "SecurityGroups": [
4         {
5             "IpPermissionsEgress": [],
6             "Description": "My security group"
7             "IpPermissions": [
8                 {
9                     "ToPort": 22,
```

75

```
10          "IpProtocol": "tcp",
11          "IpRanges": [
12              {
13                  "CidrIp": "203.0.113.0/24"
14              }
15          ]
16          "UserIdGroupPairs": [],
17          "FromPort": 22
18      }
19  ],
20  "GroupName": "my-sg",
21  "OwnerId": "123456789012",
22  "GroupId": "sg-903004f8"
23      }
24  ]
25 }
```

Deleting Your Security Group

To delete a security group, use the delete-security-group command. Note that you can't delete a security group if it is attached to an environment.

EC2-VPC

The following command deletes the security group with the ID sg-903004f8:

```
1 $ aws ec2 delete-security-group --group-id sg-903004f8
```

EC2-Classic

The following command deletes the security group named my-sg:

```
1 $ aws ec2 delete-security-group --group-name my-sg
```

Using Amazon EC2 Instances

You can use the AWS CLI to launch, list, and terminate instances. You'll need a key pair and a security group; for information about creating these through the AWS CLI, see Using Key Pairs and Using Security Groups. You'll also need to select an Amazon Machine Image (AMI) and note its AMI ID. For more information, see Finding a Suitable AMI in the *Amazon EC2 User Guide for Linux Instances*.

If you launch an instance that is not within the Free Usage Tier, you are billed after you launch the instance and charged for the time that the instance is running, even if it remains idle.

Note
Before you try the example command, set your default credentials.

- Launching an Instance
- Adding a Block Device Mapping to Your Instance
- Adding a Name Tag to Your Instance
- Connecting to Your Instance
- Listing Your Instances
- Terminating Your Instance

Launching an Instance

To launch a single Amazon EC2 instance using the AMI you selected, use the run-instances command. Depending on the platforms that your account supports, you can launch the instance into EC2-Classic or EC2-VPC.

Initially, your instance is in the **pending** state, but will be in the **running** state in a few minutes.

EC2-VPC

The following command launches a `t1.micro` instance in the specified subnet:

```
1 $ aws ec2 run-instances --image-id
2          ami-xxxxxxxx --count 1 --instance-type t2.micro --key-name MyKeyPair --security-group-
               ids sg-xxxxxxxx --subnet-id subnet-xxxxxxxx
3 {
4      "OwnerId": "123456789012",
5      "ReservationId": "r-5875ca20",
6      "Groups": [
7          {
8              "GroupName": "my-sg",
9              "GroupId": "sg-903004f8"
10         }
11     ],
12     "Instances": [
13         {
14             "Monitoring": {
15                 "State": "disabled"
16             },
17             "PublicDnsName": null,
18             "Platform": "windows",
19             "State": {
20                 "Code": 0,
21                 "Name": "pending"
22             },
23             "EbsOptimized": false,
```

```
24          "LaunchTime": "2013-07-19T02:42:39.000Z",
25          "PrivateIpAddress": "10.0.1.114",
26          "ProductCodes": [],
27          "VpcId": "vpc-1a2b3c4d",
28          "InstanceId": "i-5203422c",
29          "ImageId": "ami-173d747e",
30          "PrivateDnsName": ip-10-0-1-114.ec2.internal,
31          "KeyName": "MyKeyPair",
32          "SecurityGroups": [
33              {
34                  "GroupName": "my-sg",
35                  "GroupId": "sg-903004f8"
36              }
37          ],
38          "ClientToken": null,
39          "SubnetId": "subnet-6e7f829e",
40          "InstanceType": "t2.micro",
41          "NetworkInterfaces": [
42              {
43                  "Status": "in-use",
44                  "SourceDestCheck": true,
45                  "VpcId": "vpc-1a2b3c4d",
46                  "Description": "Primary network interface",
47                  "NetworkInterfaceId": "eni-a7edb1c9",
48                  "PrivateIpAddresses": [
49                      {
50                          "PrivateDnsName": "ip-10-0-1-114.ec2.internal",
51                          "Primary": true,
52                          "PrivateIpAddress": "10.0.1.114"
53                      }
54                  ],
55                  "PrivateDnsName": "ip-10-0-1-114.ec2.internal",
56                  "Attachment": {
57                      "Status": "attached",
58                      "DeviceIndex": 0,
59                      "DeleteOnTermination": true,
60                      "AttachmentId": "eni-attach-52193138",
61                      "AttachTime": "2013-07-19T02:42:39.000Z"
62                  },
63                  "Groups": [
64                      {
65                          "GroupName": "my-sg",
66                          "GroupId": "sg-903004f8"
67                      }
68                  ],
69                  "SubnetId": "subnet-6e7f829e",
70                  "OwnerId": "123456789012",
71                  "PrivateIpAddress": "10.0.1.114"
72              }
73          ],
74          "SourceDestCheck": true,
75          "Placement": {
76              "Tenancy": "default",
77              "GroupName": null,
```

```
 78                "AvailabilityZone": "us-west-2b"
 79            },
 80            "Hypervisor": "xen",
 81            "BlockDeviceMappings": [
 82                {
 83                    "DeviceName": "/dev/sda1",
 84                    "Ebs": {
 85                        "Status": "attached",
 86                        "DeleteOnTermination": true,
 87                        "VolumeId": "vol-877166c8",
 88                        "AttachTime": "2013-07-19T02:42:39.000Z"
 89                    }
 90                }
 91            ],
 92            "Architecture": "x86_64",
 93            "StateReason": {
 94                "Message": "pending",
 95                "Code": "pending"
 96            },
 97            "RootDeviceName": "/dev/sda1",
 98            "VirtualizationType": "hvm",
 99            "RootDeviceType": "ebs",
100            "Tags": [
101                {
102                    "Value": "MyInstance",
103                    "Key": "Name"
104                }
105            ],
106            "AmiLaunchIndex": 0
107        }
108    ]
109 }
```

EC2-Classic

The following command launches a `t1.micro` instance in EC2-Classic:

```
 1 $ aws ec2 run-instances --image-id ami-xxxxxxxx --count 1 --instance-type t1.micro --key-name
     MyKeyPair --security-groups my-sg
 2 {
 3     "OwnerId": "123456789012",
 4     "ReservationId": "r-5875ca20",
 5     "Groups": [
 6         {
 7             "GroupName": "my-sg",
 8             "GroupId": "sg-903004f8"
 9         }
10     ],
11     "Instances": [
12         {
13             "Monitoring": {
14                 "State": "disabled"
15             },
16             "PublicDnsName": null,
```

79

```
17          "Platform": "windows",
18          "State": {
19              "Code": 0,
20              "Name": "pending"
21          },
22          "EbsOptimized": false,
23          "LaunchTime": "2013-07-19T02:42:39.000Z",
24          "ProductCodes": [],
25          "InstanceId": "i-5203422c",
26          "ImageId": "ami-173d747e",
27          "PrivateDnsName": null,
28          "KeyName": "MyKeyPair",
29          "SecurityGroups": [
30              {
31                  "GroupName": "my-sg",
32                  "GroupId": "sg-903004f8"
33              }
34          ],
35          "ClientToken": null,
36          "InstanceType": "t1.micro",
37          "NetworkInterfaces": [],
38          "Placement": {
39              "Tenancy": "default",
40              "GroupName": null,
41              "AvailabilityZone": "us-west-2b"
42          },
43          "Hypervisor": "xen",
44          "BlockDeviceMappings": [
45              {
46                  "DeviceName": "/dev/sda1",
47                  "Ebs": {
48                      "Status": "attached",
49                      "DeleteOnTermination": true,
50                      "VolumeId": "vol-877166c8",
51                      "AttachTime": "2013-07-19T02:42:39.000Z"
52                  }
53              }
54          ],
55          "Architecture": "x86_64",
56          "StateReason": {
57              "Message": "pending",
58              "Code": "pending"
59          },
60          "RootDeviceName": "/dev/sda1",
61          "VirtualizationType": "hvm",
62          "RootDeviceType": "ebs",
63          "Tags": [
64              {
65                  "Value": "MyInstance",
66                  "Key": "Name"
67              }
68          ],
69          "AmiLaunchIndex": 0
70      }
```

```
71      ]
72  }
```

Adding a Block Device Mapping to Your Instance

Each instance that you launch has an associated root device volume. You can use block device mapping to specify additional EBS volumes or instance store volumes to attach to an instance when it's launched.

To add a block device mapping to your instance, specify the `--block-device-mappings` option when you use `run-instances`.

The following example adds a standard Amazon EBS volume, mapped to `/dev/sdf`, that's 20 GB in size.

```
1  --block-device-mappings "[{\"DeviceName\":\"/dev/sdf\",\"Ebs\":{\"VolumeSize\":20,\"
       DeleteOnTermination\":false}}]"
```

The following example adds an Amazon EBS volume, mapped to `/dev/sdf`, based on a snapshot. When you specify a snapshot, it isn't necessary to specify a volume size, but if you do, it must be greater than or equal to the size of the snapshot.

```
1  --block-device-mappings "[{\"DeviceName\":\"/dev/sdf\",\"Ebs\":{\"SnapshotId\":\"snap-xxxxxxxx
       \"}}]"
```

The following example adds two instance store volumes. Note that the number of instance store volumes available to your instance depends on its instance type.

```
1  --block-device-mappings "[{\"DeviceName\":\"/dev/sdf\",\"VirtualName\":\"ephemeral0\"},{\"
       DeviceName\":\"/dev/sdg\",\"VirtualName\":\"ephemeral1\"}]"
```

The following example omits a mapping for a device specified by the AMI used to launch the instance (`/dev/sdj`):

```
1  --block-device-mappings "[{\"DeviceName\":\"/dev/sdj\",\"NoDevice\":\"\"}]"
```

For more information, see Block Device Mapping in the *Amazon EC2 User Guide for Linux Instances*.

Adding a Name Tag to Your Instance

To add the tag `Name=MyInstance` to your instance, use the create-tags command as follows:

```
1  $ aws ec2 create-tags --resources i-xxxxxxxx --tags Key=Name,Value=MyInstance
```

For more information, see Tagging Your Resources in the *Amazon EC2 User Guide for Linux Instances*.

Connecting to Your Instance

While your instance is running, you can connect to it and use it just as you'd use a computer sitting in front of you. For more information, see Connect to Your Amazon EC2 Instance in the *Amazon EC2 User Guide for Linux Instances*.

Listing Your Instances

You can use the AWS CLI to list your instances and view information about them. You can list all your instances, or filter the results based on the instances that you're interested in.

Note
Before you try the example commands, set your default credentials.

The following examples show how to use the describe-instances command.

Example 1: List the instances with the specified instance type
The following command lists your m1.small instances.

```
1 $ aws ec2 describe-instances --filters "Name=instance-type,Values=m1.small"
```

Example 2: List the instances launched using the specified images
The following command lists your instances that were launched from the following AMIs: ami-x0123456, ami-y0123456, and ami-z0123456.

```
1 $ aws ec2 describe-instances --filters "Name=image-id,Values=ami-x0123456,ami-y0123456,ami-
    z0123456"
```

Terminating Your Instance

Terminating an instance effectively deletes it; you can't reconnect to an instance after you've terminated it. As soon as the state of the instance changes to shutting-down or terminated, you stop incurring charges for that instance.

When you are finished with the instance, use the terminate-instances command as follows:

```
1 $ aws ec2 terminate-instances --instance-ids i-5203422c
2 {
3     "TerminatingInstances": [
4         {
5             "InstanceId": "i-5203422c",
6             "CurrentState": {
7                 "Code": 32,
8                 "Name": "shutting-down"
9             },
10            "PreviousState": {
11                "Code": 16,
12                "Name": "running"
13            }
14        }
15    ]
16 }
```

For more information, see Terminate Your Instance in the *Amazon EC2 User Guide for Linux Instances.*

Using Amazon Glacier with the AWS Command Line Interface

You can upload a large file to Amazon Glacier by splitting it into smaller parts and uploading them from the command line. This topic describes the process of creating a vault, splitting a file, and configuring and executing a multipart upload to Amazon Glacier with the AWS CLI.

Note
This tutorial uses several command line tools that typically come pre-installed on Unix-like operating systems including Linux and OS X. Windows users can use the same tools by installing Cygwin and running the commands from the Cygwin terminal. Windows native commands and utilities that perform the same functions are noted where available.

- Create an Amazon Glacier Vault
- Prepare a File for Uploading
- Initiate a Multipart Upload and Upload Files
- Complete the Upload

Create an Amazon Glacier Vault

Create a vault with the `aws glacier create-vault` command. The following command creates a vault named `myvault`.

```
1 $ aws glacier create-vault --account-id - --vault-name myvault
2 {
3     "location": "/123456789012/vaults/myvault"
4 }
```

Note
All glacier commands require an account ID parameter. Use a hyphen to specify the current account.

Prepare a File for Uploading

Create a file for the test upload. The following commands create a file that contains exactly 3 MiB (3 x 1024 x 1024 bytes) of random data.

Linux, macOS, or Unix

```
1 $ dd if=/dev/urandom of=largefile bs=3145728 count=1
2 1+0 records in
3 1+0 records out
4 3145728 bytes (3.1 MB) copied, 0.205813 s, 15.3 MB/s
```

`dd` is a utility that copies a number of bytes from an input file to an output file. The above example uses the device file `/dev/urandom` as a source of random data. `fsutil` performs a similar function in Windows:

Windows

```
1 C:\temp>fsutil file createnew largefile 3145728
2 File C:\temp\largefile is created
```

Next, split the file into 1 MiB (1048576 byte) chunks.

```
1 $ split --bytes=1048576 --verbose largefile chunk
2 creating file `chunkaa'
3 creating file `chunkab'
4 creating file `chunkac'
```

Note

HJ-Split is a free file splitter for Windows and many other platforms.

Initiate a Multipart Upload and Upload Files

Create a multipart upload in Amazon Glacier by using the `aws glacier initiate-multipart-upload` command.

```
1 $ aws glacier initiate-multipart-upload --account-id - --archive-description "multipart upload
    test" --part-size 1048576 --vault-name myvault
2 {
3     "uploadId": "19gaRezEXAMPLES6Ry5YYdqthHOC_kGRCT03L9yetr220UmPtBYKk-
        OssZtLqyFu7sY1_lR7vgFuJV6NtcV5zpsJ",
4     "location": "/123456789012/vaults/myvault/multipart-uploads/19
        gaRezEXAMPLES6Ry5YYdqthHOC_kGRCT03L9yetr220UmPtBYKk-OssZtLqyFu7sY1_lR7vgFuJV6NtcV5zpsJ"
5 }
```

Amazon Glacier requires the size of each part in bytes (1 MiB in this example), your vault name, and an account ID in order to configure the multipart upload. The AWS CLI outputs an upload ID when the operation is complete. Save the upload ID to a shell variable for later use.

Linux, macOS, or Unix

```
1 $ UPLOADID="19gaRezEXAMPLES6Ry5YYdqthHOC_kGRCT03L9yetr220UmPtBYKk-
    OssZtLqyFu7sY1_lR7vgFuJV6NtcV5zpsJ"
```

Windows

```
1 C:\temp> set UPLOADID="19gaRezEXAMPLES6Ry5YYdqthHOC_kGRCT03L9yetr220UmPtBYKk-
    OssZtLqyFu7sY1_lR7vgFuJV6NtcV5zpsJ"
```

Next, use the `aws glacier upload-multipart-part` command to upload each part.

```
1 $ aws glacier upload-multipart-part --upload-id $UPLOADID --body chunkaa --range 'bytes
    0-1048575/*' --account-id - --vault-name myvault
2 {
3     "checksum": "e1f2a7cd6e047fa606fe2f0280350f69b9f8cfa602097a9a026360a7edc1f553"
4 }
5 $ aws glacier upload-multipart-part --upload-id $UPLOADID --body chunkab --range 'bytes
    1048576-2097151/*' --account-id - --vault-name myvault
6 {
7     "checksum": "e1f2a7cd6e047fa606fe2f0280350f69b9f8cfa602097a9a026360a7edc1f553"
8 }
9 $ aws glacier upload-multipart-part --upload-id $UPLOADID --body chunkac --range 'bytes
    2097152-3145727/*' --account-id - --vault-name myvault
10 {
11     "checksum": "e1f2a7cd6e047fa606fe2f0280350f69b9f8cfa602097a9a026360a7edc1f553"
12 }
```

Note

The above example uses the dollar sign (”$”) to dereference the `UPLOADID` shell variable. On the Windows command line, use two percent signs (i.e. `%UPLOADID%`).

You must specify the byte range of each part when you upload it so it can be reassembled in the proper order by Amazon Glacier. Each piece is 1048576 bytes, so the first piece occupies bytes 0-1048575, the second 1048576-2097151, and the third 2097152-3145727.

Complete the Upload

Amazon Glacier requires a tree hash of the original file in order to confirm that all of the uploaded pieces reached AWS intact. To calculate a tree hash, you split the file into 1 MiB parts and calculate a binary SHA-256 hash of each piece. Then you split the list of hashes into pairs, combine the two binary hashes in each pair, and take hashes of the results. Repeat this process until there is only one hash left. If there is an odd number of hashes at any level, promote it to the next level without modifying it.

The key to calculating a tree hash correctly when using command line utilities is to store each hash in binary format and only convert to hexadecimal at the last step. Combining or hashing the hexadecimal version of any hash in the tree will cause an incorrect result.

Note
Windows users can use the `type` command in place of `cat`. OpenSSL is available for Windows at OpenSSL.org.

To calculate a tree hash

1. Split the original file into 1 MiB parts if you haven't already.

```
1 $ split --bytes=1048576 --verbose largefile chunk
2 creating file `chunkaa'
3 creating file `chunkab'
4 creating file `chunkac'
```

2. Calculate and store the binary SHA-256 hash of each chunk.

```
1 $ openssl dgst -sha256 -binary chunkaa > hash1
2 $ openssl dgst -sha256 -binary chunkab > hash2
3 $ openssl dgst -sha256 -binary chunkac > hash3
```

3. Combine the first two hashes and take the binary hash of the result.

```
1 $ cat hash1 hash2 > hash12
2 $ openssl dgst -sha256 -binary hash12 > hash12hash
```

4. Combine the parent hash of chunks aa and ab with the hash of chunk ac and hash the result, this time outputing hexadecimal. Store the result in a shell variable.

```
1 $ cat hash12hash hash3 > hash123
2 $ openssl dgst -sha256 hash123
3 SHA256(hash123)= 9628195fcdbcbbe76cdde932d4646fa7de5f219fb39823836d81f0cc0e18aa67
4 $ TREEHASH=9628195fcdbcbbe76cdde932d4646fa7de5f219fb39823836d81f0cc0e18aa67
```

Finally, complete the upload with the **aws glacier complete-multipart-upload** command. This command takes the original file's size in bytes, the final tree hash value in hexadecimal, and your account ID and vault name.

```
1 $ aws glacier complete-multipart-upload --checksum $TREEHASH --archive-size 3145728 --upload-id
      $UPLOADID --account-id - --vault-name myvault
2 {
3     "archiveId": "d3AbWhEOYE1m6f_fI1jPG82F8xzbMEEZmrAlLGAAONJAzo5QdP-N83MKqd96Unspoa5H5lItWX-sK8
          -QSOZhwsyGiu9-R-kwWUyS1dSBlmgPPWkEbeFfqDSav053rU7FvVLHfRc6hg",
4     "checksum": "9628195fcdbcbbe76cdde932d4646fa7de5f219fb39823836d81f0cc0e18aa67",
5     "location": "/123456789012/vaults/myvault/archives/
          d3AbWhEOYE1m6f_fI1jPG82F8xzbMEEZmrAlLGAAONJAzo5QdP-N83MKqd96Unspoa5H5lItWX-sK8-
          QSOZhwsyGiu9-R-kwWUyS1dSBlmgPPWkEbeFfqDSav053rU7FvVLHfRc6hg"
6 }
```

You can also check the status of the vault using **aws glacier describe-vault**:

```
1 $ aws glacier describe-vault --account-id - --vault-name myvault
2 {
3     "SizeInBytes": 3178496,
4     "VaultARN": "arn:aws:glacier:us-west-2:123456789012:vaults/myvault",
5     "LastInventoryDate": "2015-04-07T00:26:19.028Z",
6     "NumberOfArchives": 1,
7     "CreationDate": "2015-04-06T21:23:45.708Z",
8     "VaultName": "myvault"
9 }
```

Note

Vault status is updated about once per day. See Working with Vaults for more information

It is now safe to remove the part and hash files you created:

```
1 $ rm chunk* hash*
```

For more information on multipart uploads, see Uploading Large Archives in Parts and Computing Checksums in the Amazon Glacier Developer Guide.

AWS Identity and Access Management from the AWS Command Line Interface

This section describes some common tasks related to AWS Identity and Access Management (IAM) and how to perform them using the AWS Command Line Interface.

The commands shown here assume that you have set default credentials and a default region.

- Create New IAM Users and Groups
- Set an IAM Policy for an IAM User
- Set an Initial Password for an IAM User
- Create Security Credentials for an IAM User

Create New IAM Users and Groups

This section describes how to create a new IAM group and a new IAM user and then add the user to the group.

To create an IAM group and add a new IAM user to it

1. First, use the `create-group` command to create the group.

```
1  $ aws iam create-group --group-name MyIamGroup
2  {
3      "Group": {
4          "GroupName": "MyIamGroup",
5          "CreateDate": "2012-12-20T03:03:52.834Z",
6          "GroupId": "AKIAI44QH8DHBEXAMPLE",
7          "Arn": "arn:aws:iam::123456789012:group/MyIamGroup",
8          "Path": "/"
9      }
10 }
```

2. Next, use the `create-user` command to create the user.

```
1  $ aws iam create-user --user-name MyUser
2  {
3      "User": {
4          "UserName": "MyUser",
5          "Path": "/",
6          "CreateDate": "2012-12-20T03:13:02.581Z",
7          "UserId": "AKIAIOSFODNN7EXAMPLE",
8          "Arn": "arn:aws:iam::123456789012:user/MyUser"
9      }
10 }
```

3. Finally, use the `add-user-to-group` command to add the user to the group.

```
1  $ aws iam add-user-to-group --user-name MyUser --group-name MyIamGroup
```

4. To verify that the `MyIamGroup` group contains the `MyUser`, use the `get-group` command.

```
1  $ aws iam get-group --group-name MyIamGroup
2  {
3      "Group": {
4          "GroupName": "MyIamGroup",
5          "CreateDate": "2012-12-20T03:03:52Z",
6          "GroupId": "AKIAI44QH8DHBEXAMPLE",
7          "Arn": "arn:aws:iam::123456789012:group/MyIamGroup",
8          "Path": "/"
9      },
10     "Users": [
11         {
12             "UserName": "MyUser",
13             "Path": "/",
14             "CreateDate": "2012-12-20T03:13:02Z",
15             "UserId": "AKIAIOSFODNN7EXAMPLE",
16             "Arn": "arn:aws:iam::123456789012:user/MyUser"
17         }
18     ],
19     "IsTruncated": "false"
20 }
```

You can also view IAM users and groups with the AWS Management Console.

Set an IAM Policy for an IAM User

The following commands show how to assign an IAM policy to an IAM user. The policy specified here provides the user with "Power User Access". This policy is identical to the **Power User Access** policy template provided in the IAM console. In this example, the policy is saved to a file, `MyPolicyFile.json`:

```
1  {
2    "Version": "2012-10-17",
3    "Statement": [
4      {
5        "Effect": "Allow",
6        "NotAction": "iam:*",
7        "Resource": "*"
8      }
9    ]
10 }
```

To specify the policy, use the `put-user-policy` command.

```
1  $ aws iam put-user-policy --user-name MyUser --policy-name MyPowerUserRole --policy-document
     file://C:\Temp\MyPolicyFile.json
```

Verify the policy has been assigned to the user with the `list-user-policies` command.

```
1  $ aws iam list-user-policies --user-name MyUser
2  {
3      "PolicyNames": [
4          "MyPowerUserRole"
5      ],
6      "IsTruncated": "false"
7  }
```

Additional Resources

For more information, see Resources for Learning About Permissions and Policies. This topic provides links to an overview of permissions and policies and links to examples of policies for accessing Amazon S3, Amazon EC2, and other services.

Set an Initial Password for an IAM User

The following example demonstrates how to use the `create-login-profile` command to set an initial password for an IAM user.

```
1 $ aws iam create-login-profile --user-name MyUser --password My!User1Login8P@ssword
2 {
3     "LoginProfile": {
4         "UserName": "MyUser",
5         "CreateDate": "2013-01-02T21:10:54.339Z",
6         "MustChangePassword": "false"
7     }
8 }
```

Use the `update-login-profile` command to update the password for an IAM user.

Create Security Credentials for an IAM User

The following example uses the `create-access-key` command to create security credentials for an IAM user. A set of security credentials comprises an access key ID and a secret key. Note that an IAM user can have no more than two sets of credentials at any given time. If you attempt to create a third set, the `create-access-key` command will return a "LimitExceeded" error.

```
1  $ aws iam create-access-key --user-name MyUser
2  {
3      "AccessKey": {
4          "SecretAccessKey": "je7MtGbClwBF/2Zp9Utk/h3yCo8nvbEXAMPLEKEY",
5          "Status": "Active",
6          "CreateDate": "2013-01-02T22:44:12.897Z",
7          "UserName": "MyUser",
8          "AccessKeyId": "AKIAI44QH8DHBEXAMPLE"
9      }
10 }
```

Use the `delete-access-key` command to delete a set of credentials for an IAM user. Specify which credentials to delete by using the access key ID.

```
1  $ aws iam delete-access-key --user-name MyUser --access-key-id AKIAI44QH8DHBEXAMPLE
```

Using Amazon S3 with the AWS Command Line Interface

The AWS CLI provides two tiers of commands for accessing Amazon S3.

- The first tier, named *s3*, consists of high-level commands for frequently used operations, such as creating, manipulating, and deleting objects and buckets.

- The second tier, named *s3api*, exposes all Amazon S3 operations, including modifying a bucket access control list (ACL), using cross-origin resource sharing (CORS), or logging policies. It allows you to carry out advanced operations that may not be possible with the high-level commands alone.

To get a list of all commands available in each tier, use the `help` argument with the `aws s3` or `aws s3api` commands:

```
1 $ aws s3 help
```

or

```
1 $ aws s3api help
```

Note

The AWS CLI supports copying, moving, and syncing from Amazon S3 to Amazon S3. These operations use the *service-side* COPY operation provided by Amazon S3: Your files are kept in the cloud, and are *not* downloaded to the client machine, then back up to Amazon S3.

When operations such as these can be performed completely in the cloud, only the bandwidth necessary for the HTTP request and response is used.

For examples of Amazon S3 usage, see the following topics in this section.

- Using High-Level s3 Commands with the AWS Command Line Interface
- Using API-Level (s3api) Commands with the AWS Command Line Interface

Using High-Level s3 Commands with the AWS Command Line Interface

This section describes how you can manage Amazon S3 buckets and objects using high-level `aws s3` commands.

Managing Buckets

High-level `aws s3` commands support commonly used bucket operations, such as creating, removing, and listing buckets.

Creating Buckets

Use the `aws s3 mb` command to create a new bucket. Bucket names must be unique and should be DNS compliant. Bucket names can contain lowercase letters, numbers, hyphens and periods. Bucket names can only start and end with a letter or number, and cannot contain a period next to a hyphen or another period.

```
1 $ aws s3 mb s3://bucket-name
```

Removing Buckets

To remove a bucket, use the `aws s3 rb` command.

```
1 $ aws s3 rb s3://bucket-name
```

By default, the bucket must be empty for the operation to succeed. To remove a non-empty bucket, you need to include the `--force` option.

```
1 $ aws s3 rb s3://bucket-name --force
```

This will first delete all objects and subfolders in the bucket and then remove the bucket.

Note
If you are using a versioned bucket that contains previously deleted—but retained—objects, this command will *not* allow you to remove the bucket.

Listing Buckets

To list all buckets or their contents, use the `aws s3 ls` command. Here are some examples of common usage.

The following command lists all buckets.

```
1 $ aws s3 ls
2 2013-07-11 17:08:50 my-bucket
3 2013-07-24 14:55:44 my-bucket2
```

The following command lists all objects and folders (prefixes) in a bucket.

```
1 $ aws s3 ls s3://bucket-name
2                           PRE path/
3 2013-09-04 19:05:48          3 MyFile1.txt
```

The following command lists the objects in *bucket-name*/`path` (in other words, objects in *bucket-name* filtered by the prefix `path/`).

```
1 $ aws s3 ls s3://bucket-name/path/
2 2013-09-06 18:59:32          3 MyFile2.txt
```

Managing Objects

The high-level `aws s3` commands make it convenient to manage Amazon S3 objects as well. The object commands include `aws s3 cp`, `aws s3 ls`, `aws s3 mv`, `aws s3 rm`, and `sync`. The `cp`, `ls`, `mv`, and `rm` commands work similarly to their Unix counterparts and enable you to work seamlessly across your local directories and Amazon S3 buckets. The `sync` command synchronizes the contents of a bucket and a directory, or two buckets.

Note
All high-level commands that involve uploading objects into an Amazon S3 bucket (`aws s3 cp`, `aws s3 mv`, and `aws s3 sync`) automatically perform a multipart upload when the object is large.

Failed uploads cannot be resumed when using these commands. If the multipart upload fails due to a timeout or is manually cancelled by pressing CTRL+C, the AWS CLI cleans up any files created and aborts the upload. This process can take several minutes.

If the process is interrupted by a kill command or system failure, the in-progress multipart upload remains in Amazon S3 and must be cleaned up manually in the AWS Management Console or with the s3api abort-multipart-upload command.

The `cp`, `mv`, and `sync` commands include a `--grants` option that can be used to grant permissions on the object to specified users or groups. You set the `--grants` option to a list of permissions using following syntax:

```
1 --grants Permission=Grantee_Type=Grantee_ID
2          [Permission=Grantee_Type=Grantee_ID ...]
```

Each value contains the following elements:

- *Permission* – Specifies the granted permissions, and can be set to `read`, `readacl`, `writeacl`, or `full`.

- *Grantee_Type* – Specifies how the grantee is to be identified, and can be set to `uri`, `emailaddress`, or `id`.

- *Grantee_ID* – Specifies the grantee based on *Grantee_Type*.

    - `uri` – The group's URI. For more information, see Who Is a Grantee?

    - `emailaddress` – The account's email address.

    - `id` – The account's canonical ID.

For more information on Amazon S3 access control, see Access Control.

The following example copies an object into a bucket. It grants `read` permissions on the object to everyone and `full` permissions (`read`, `readacl`, and `writeacl`) to the account associated with `user@example.com`.

```
1 $ aws s3 cp file.txt s3://my-bucket/ --grants read=uri=http://acs.amazonaws.com/groups/global/
    AllUsers full=emailaddress=user@example.com
```

To specify a non-default storage class (`REDUCED_REDUNDANCY` or `STANDARD_IA`) for objects that you upload to Amazon S3, use the `--storage-class` option:

```
1 $ aws s3 cp file.txt s3://my-bucket/ --storage-class REDUCED_REDUNDANCY
```

The `sync` command has the following form. Possible source-target combinations are:

- Local file system to Amazon S3

- Amazon S3 to local file system

- Amazon S3 to Amazon S3

```
1 $ aws s3 sync <source> <target> [--options]
```

The following example synchronizes the contents of an Amazon S3 folder named *path* in *my-bucket* with the current working directory. s3 sync updates any files that have a different size or modified time than files with the same name at the destination. The output displays specific operations performed during the sync. Notice that the operation recursively synchronizes the subdirectory *MySubdirectory* and its contents with *s3://my-bucket/path/MySubdirectory*.

```
1 $ aws s3 sync . s3://my-bucket/path
2 upload: MySubdirectory\MyFile3.txt to s3://my-bucket/path/MySubdirectory/MyFile3.txt
3 upload: MyFile2.txt to s3://my-bucket/path/MyFile2.txt
4 upload: MyFile1.txt to s3://my-bucket/path/MyFile1.txt
```

Normally, sync only copies missing or outdated files or objects between the source and target. However, you may supply the --delete option to remove files or objects from the target not present in the source.

The following example, which extends the previous one, shows how this works.

```
1 // Delete local file
2 $ rm ./MyFile1.txt
3
4 // Attempt sync without --delete option - nothing happens
5 $ aws s3 sync . s3://my-bucket/path
6
7 // Sync with deletion - object is deleted from bucket
8 $ aws s3 sync . s3://my-bucket/path --delete
9 delete: s3://my-bucket/path/MyFile1.txt
10
11 // Delete object from bucket
12 $ aws s3 rm s3://my-bucket/path/MySubdirectory/MyFile3.txt
13 delete: s3://my-bucket/path/MySubdirectory/MyFile3.txt
14
15 // Sync with deletion - local file is deleted
16 $ aws s3 sync s3://my-bucket/path . --delete
17 delete: MySubdirectory\MyFile3.txt
18
19 // Sync with Infrequent Access storage class
20 $ aws s3 sync . s3://my-bucket/path --storage-class STANDARD_IA
```

The --exclude and --include options allow you to specify rules to filter the files or objects to be copied during the sync operation. By default, all items in a specified directory are included in the sync. Therefore, --include is only needed when specifying exceptions to the --exclude option (for example, --include effectively means "don't exclude"). The options apply in the order that is specified, as demonstrated in the following example.

```
1 Local directory contains 3 files:
2 MyFile1.txt
3 MyFile2.rtf
4 MyFile88.txt
5 '''
6 $ aws s3 sync . s3://my-bucket/path --exclude '*.txt'
7 upload: MyFile2.rtf to s3://my-bucket/path/MyFile2.rtf
8 '''
9 $ aws s3 sync . s3://my-bucket/path --exclude '*.txt' --include 'MyFile*.txt'
10 upload: MyFile1.txt to s3://my-bucket/path/MyFile1.txt
11 upload: MyFile88.txt to s3://my-bucket/path/MyFile88.txt
12 upload: MyFile2.rtf to s3://my-bucket/path/MyFile2.rtf
13 '''
14 $ aws s3 sync . s3://my-bucket/path --exclude '*.txt' --include 'MyFile*.txt' --exclude 'MyFile
     ?.txt'
```

96

```
15 upload: MyFile2.rtf to s3://my-bucket/path/MyFile2.rtf
16 upload: MyFile88.txt to s3://my-bucket/path/MyFile88.txt
```

The `--exclude` and `--include` options can also filter files or objects to be deleted during a sync operation with the `--delete` option. In this case, the parameter string must specify files to be excluded from, or included for, deletion in the context of the target directory or bucket. The following shows an example.

```
1 Assume local directory and s3://my-bucket/path currently in sync and each contains 3 files:
2 MyFile1.txt
3 MyFile2.rtf
4 MyFile88.txt
5 '''
6 // Delete local .txt files
7 $ rm *.txt
8
9 // Sync with delete, excluding files that match a pattern. MyFile88.txt is deleted, while remote
       MyFile1.txt is not.
10 $ aws s3 sync . s3://my-bucket/path --delete --exclude 'my-bucket/path/MyFile?.txt'
11 delete: s3://my-bucket/path/MyFile88.txt
12 '''
13 // Delete MyFile2.rtf
14 $ aws s3 rm s3://my-bucket/path/MyFile2.rtf
15
16 // Sync with delete, excluding MyFile2.rtf - local file is NOT deleted
17 $ aws s3 sync s3://my-bucket/path . --delete --exclude './MyFile2.rtf'
18 download: s3://my-bucket/path/MyFile1.txt to MyFile1.txt
19 '''
20 // Sync with delete, local copy of MyFile2.rtf is deleted
21 $ aws s3 sync s3://my-bucket/path . --delete
22 delete: MyFile2.rtf
```

The `sync` command also accepts an `--acl` option, by which you may set the access permissions for files copied to Amazon S3. The option accepts `private`, `public-read`, and `public-read-write` values.

```
1 $ aws s3 sync . s3://my-bucket/path --acl public-read
```

As previously mentioned, the s3 command set includes `cp`, `mv`, `ls`, and `rm`, and they work in similar ways to their Unix counterparts. The following are some examples.

```
1 // Copy MyFile.txt in current directory to s3://my-bucket/path
2 $ aws s3 cp MyFile.txt s3://my-bucket/path/
3
4 // Move all .jpg files in s3://my-bucket/path to ./MyDirectory
5 $ aws s3 mv s3://my-bucket/path ./MyDirectory --exclude '*' --include '*.jpg' --recursive
6
7 // List the contents of my-bucket
8 $ aws s3 ls s3://my-bucket
9
10 // List the contents of path in my-bucket
11 $ aws s3 ls s3://my-bucket/path/
12
13 // Delete s3://my-bucket/path/MyFile.txt
14 $ aws s3 rm s3://my-bucket/path/MyFile.txt
15
16 // Delete s3://my-bucket/path and all of its contents
17 $ aws s3 rm s3://my-bucket/path --recursive
```

When the `--recursive` option is used on a directory/folder with `cp`, `mv`, or `rm`, the command walks the directory tree, including all subdirectories. These commands also accept the `--exclude`, `--include`, and `--acl` options as the `sync` command does.

Using API-Level (s3api) Commands with the AWS Command Line Interface

The API-level commands (contained in the **s3api** command set) provide direct access to the Amazon S3 APIs and enable some operations not exposed in the high-level commands. This section describes the API-level commands and provides a few examples. For more Amazon S3 examples, see the s3api command-line reference and choose an available command from the list.

Custom ACLs

With high-level commands, you can use the **--acl** option to apply pre-defined access control lists (ACLs) on Amazon S3 objects, but you cannot set bucket-wide ACLs. You can do this with the API-level command, **put-bucket-acl**. The following example grants full control to two AWS users (*user1@example.com* and *user2@example.com*) and read permission to everyone.

```
1 $ aws s3api put-bucket-acl --bucket MyBucket --grant-full-control 'emailaddress="user1@example.
    com",emailaddress="user2@example.com"' --grant-read 'uri="http://acs.amazonaws.com/groups/
    global/AllUsers"'
```

For details about custom ACLs, see PUT Bucket acl. The **s3api** ACL commands, such as **put-bucket-acl**, use the same shorthand argument notation.

Logging Policy

The API command **put-bucket-logging** configures bucket logging policy. The following example sets the logging policy for *MyBucket*. The AWS user *user@example.com* will have full control over the log files, and all users will have access to them. Note that the **put-bucket-acl** command is required to grant Amazon S3's log delivery system the necessary permissions (write and read-acp).

```
1 $ aws s3api put-bucket-acl --bucket MyBucket --grant-write 'URI="http://acs.amazonaws.com/groups
    /s3/LogDelivery"' --grant-read-acp 'URI="http://acs.amazonaws.com/groups/s3/LogDelivery"'
2 $ aws s3api put-bucket-logging --bucket MyBucket --bucket-logging-status file://logging.json
```

logging.json

```
1  {
2    "LoggingEnabled": {
3      "TargetBucket": "MyBucket",
4      "TargetPrefix": "MyBucketLogs/",
5      "TargetGrants": [
6        {
7          "Grantee": {
8            "Type": "AmazonCustomerByEmail",
9            "EmailAddress": "user@example.com"
10         },
11         "Permission": "FULL_CONTROL"
12       },
13       {
14         "Grantee": {
15           "Type": "Group",
16           "URI": "http://acs.amazonaws.com/groups/global/AllUsers"
17         },
18         "Permission": "READ"
```

```
19          }
20       ]
21    }
22 }
```

Using the AWS Command Line Interface with Amazon SNS

This section describes some common tasks related to Amazon Simple Notification Service (Amazon SNS) and how to perform them using the AWS Command Line Interface.

- Create a Topic
- Subscribe to a Topic
- Publish to a Topic
- Unsubscribe from a Topic
- Delete a Topic

Create a Topic

The following command creates a topic named **my-topic**:

```
1 $ aws sns create-topic --name my-topic
2 {
3     "TopicArn": "arn:aws:sns:us-west-2:123456789012:my-topic"
4 }
```

Make a note of the `TopicArn`, which you will use later to publish a message.

Subscribe to a Topic

The following command subscribes to a topic using the email protocol and an email address for the notification endpoint:

```
1 $ aws sns subscribe --topic-arn arn:aws:sns:us-west-2:123456789012:my-topic --protocol email --
      notification-endpoint emailusername@example.com
2 {
3     "SubscriptionArn": "pending confirmation"
4 }
```

An email message will be sent to the email address listed in the subscribe command. The email message will have the following text:

```
1 You have chosen to subscribe to the topic:
2 arn:aws:sns:us-west-2:123456789012:my-topic
3 To confirm this subscription, click or visit the following link (If this was in error no action
      is necessary):
4 Confirm subscription
```

After clicking **Confirm subscription**, a "Subscription confirmed!" notification message should appear in your browser with information similar to the following:

```
1 Subscription confirmed!
2
3 You have subscribed emailusername@example.com to the topic:my-topic.
4
5 Your subscription's id is:
6 arn:aws:sns:us-west-2:123456789012:my-topic:1328f057-de93-4c15-512e-8bb2268db8c4
7
8 If it was not your intention to subscribe, click here to unsubscribe.
```

Publish to a Topic

The following command publishes a message to a topic:

```
1 $ aws sns publish --topic-arn arn:aws:sns:us-west-2:123456789012:my-topic --message "Hello World
    !"
2 {
3     "MessageId": "4e41661d-5eec-5ddf-8dab-2c867a709bab"
4 }
```

An email message with the text "Hello World!" will be sent to emailusername@example.com

Unsubscribe from a Topic

The following command unsubscribes from a topic:

```
1 $ aws sns unsubscribe --subscription-arn arn:aws:sns:us-west-2:123456789012:my-topic:1328f057-
    de93-4c15-512e-8bb2268db8c4
```

To verify the unsubscription to the topic, type the following:

```
1 $ aws sns list-subscriptions
```

Delete a Topic

The following command deletes a topic:

```
1 $ aws sns delete-topic --topic-arn arn:aws:sns:us-west-2:123456789012:my-topic
```

To verify the deletion of the topic, type the following:

```
1 $ aws sns list-topics
```

Using Amazon Simple Workflow Service with the AWS Command Line Interface

You can access features of Amazon Simple Workflow Service (Amazon SWF) using the AWS CLI.

For a list of commands and how to work with domains in Amazon SWF, see the following topics.

- List of Amazon SWF Commands by Category
- Working with Amazon SWF Domains Using the AWS Command Line Interface

List of Amazon SWF Commands by Category

This section lists the reference topics for Amazon SWF commands in the AWS CLI. The commands here are listed by *functional category*.

For an *alphabetic* list of commands, see the Amazon SWF section of the *AWS Command Line Interface Reference*, or use the following command.

```
1 $ aws swf help
```

To get help for a particular command, use the `help` directive after the command name. The following shows an example.

```
1 $ aws swf register-domain help
```

- Commands Related to Activities
- Commands Related to Deciders
- Commands Related to Workflow Executions
- Commands Related to Administration
- Visibility Commands

Commands Related to Activities

Activity workers use `poll-for-activity-task` to get new activity tasks. After a worker receives an activity task from Amazon SWF, it performs the task and responds using `respond-activity-task-completed` if successful or `respond-activity-task-failed` if unsuccessful.

The following are commands that are performed by activity workers.

- poll-for-activity-task

- respond-activity-task-completed

- respond-activity-task-failed

- respond-activity-task-canceled

- record-activity-task-heartbeat

Commands Related to Deciders

Deciders use `poll-for-decision-task` to get decision tasks. After a decider receives a decision task from Amazon SWF, it examines its workflow execution history and decides what to do next. It calls `respond-decision-task-completed` to complete the decision task and provides zero or more next decisions.

The following are commands that are performed by deciders.

- poll-for-decision-task

- respond-decision-task-completed

Commands Related to Workflow Executions

The following commands operate on a workflow execution.

- request-cancel-workflow-execution

- start-workflow-execution

- signal-workflow-execution
- terminate-workflow-execution

Commands Related to Administration

Although you can perform administrative tasks from the Amazon SWF console, you can use the commands in this section to automate functions or build your own administrative tools.

Activity Management

- register-activity-type
- deprecate-activity-type

Workflow Management

- register-workflow-type
- deprecate-workflow-type

Domain Management

- register-domain
- deprecate-domain

For more information and examples of these domain management commands, see .

Workflow Execution Management

- request-cancel-workflow-execution
- terminate-workflow-execution

Visibility Commands

Although you can perform visibility actions from the Amazon SWF console, you can use the commands in this section to build your own console or administrative tools.

Activity Visibility

- list-activity-types
- describe-activity-type

Workflow Visibility

- list-workflow-types
- describe-workflow-type

Workflow Execution Visibility

- describe-workflow-execution
- list-open-workflow-executions
- list-closed-workflow-executions
- count-open-workflow-executions
- count-closed-workflow-executions
- get-workflow-execution-history

Domain Visibility

- list-domains
- describe-domain

For more information and examples of these domain visibility commands, see .

Task List Visibility

- count-pending-activity-tasks
- count-pending-decision-tasks

Working with Amazon SWF Domains Using the AWS Command Line Interface

This section describes how to perform common Amazon SWF domain tasks using the AWS CLI.

- Listing Your Domains
- Getting Information About a Domain
- Registering a Domain
- Deprecating a Domain
- See Also

Listing Your Domains

To list the Amazon SWF domains that you have registered for your account, you can use `swf list-domains`. There is only one required parameter: `--registration-status`, which you can set to either `REGISTERED` or `DEPRECATED`.

Here's a minimal example:

```
1  $ aws swf list-domains --registration-status REGISTERED
2  {
3      "domainInfos": [
4          {
5              "status": "REGISTERED",
6              "name": "ExampleDomain"
7          },
8          {
9              "status": "REGISTERED",
10             "name": "mytest"
11         }
12     ]
13 }
```

Note
For an example of using `DEPRECATED`, see Deprecating a Domain. As you might guess, it returns any deprecated domains you have.

Setting a Page Size to Limit Results

If you have many domains, you can set the `--maximum-page-size` parameter to limit the number of results returned. If you get more results than the maximum number that you specified, you will receive a `nextPageToken` that you can send to the next call to `list-domains` to retrieve additional entries.

Here's an example of using `--maximum-page-size`:

```
1  $ aws swf list-domains --registration-status REGISTERED --maximum-page-size 1
2  {
3      "domainInfos": [
4          {
5              "status": "REGISTERED",
6              "name": "ExampleDomain"
7          }
8      ],
9      "nextPageToken": "ANeXAMPLEtOKENiSpRETTYlONG=="
10 }
```

Note

The `nextPageToken` that is returned to you will be much longer. This value is merely an example for illustrative purposes.

When you make the call again, this time supplying the value of `nextPageToken` in the `--next-page-token` argument, you'll get another page of results:

```
1 $ aws swf list-domains --registration-status REGISTERED --maximum-page-size 1 --next-page-token
    "ANeXAMPLEtOKENiSpRETTYlONG=="
2 {
3    "domainInfos": [
4        {
5            "status": "REGISTERED",
6            "name": "mytest"
7        }
8    ]
9 }
```

When there are no further pages of results to retrieve, `nextPageToken` will not be returned in the results.

Getting Information About a Domain

To get detailed information about a particular domain, use `swf describe-domain`. There is one required parameter: `--name`, which takes the name of the domain you want information about. For example:

```
1 $ aws swf describe-domain --name ExampleDomain
2 {
3    "domainInfo": {
4        "status": "REGISTERED",
5        "name": "ExampleDomain"
6    },
7    "configuration": {
8        "workflowExecutionRetentionPeriodInDays": "1"
9    }
10 }
```

Registering a Domain

To register new domains, use `swf register-domain`. There are two required parameters, `--name`, which takes the domain name, and `--workflow-execution-retention-period-in-days`, which takes an integer to specify the number of days to retain workflow execution data on this domain, up to a maximum period of 90 days (for more information, see the Amazon SWF FAQ). If you specify zero (0) for this value, the retention period is automatically set at the maximum duration. Otherwise, workflow execution data will not be retained after the specified number of days have passed.

Here's an example of registering a new domain:

```
1 $ aws swf register-domain --name MyNeatNewDomain --workflow-execution-retention-period-in-days 0
```

When you register a domain, nothing is returned (""), but you can use `swf list-domains` or `swf describe-domain` to see the new domain. For example:

```
1 $ aws swf list-domains --registration-status REGISTERED
2 {
3    "domainInfos": [
4        {
```

```
 5            "status": "REGISTERED",
 6            "name": "ExampleDomain"
 7        },
 8        {
 9            "status": "REGISTERED",
10            "name": "MyNeatNewDomain"
11        },
12        {
13            "status": "REGISTERED",
14            "name": "mytest"
15        }
16    ]
17 }
```

Here's an example using `swf describe-domain`:

```
 1 $ aws swf describe-domain --name MyNeatNewDomain
 2 {
 3    "domainInfo": {
 4        "status": "REGISTERED",
 5        "name": "MyNeatNewDomain"
 6    },
 7    "configuration": {
 8        "workflowExecutionRetentionPeriodInDays": "0"
 9    }
10 }
```

Deprecating a Domain

To deprecate a domain (you can still see it, but cannot create new workflow executions or register types on it), use `swf deprecate-domain`. It has a sole required parameter, `--name`, which takes the name of the domain to deprecate.

```
 1 $ aws swf deprecate-domain --name MyNeatNewDomain
```

As with `register-domain`, no output is returned. If you use `list-domains` to view the registered domains, however, you will see that the domain no longer appears among them.

```
 1 $ aws swf list-domains --registration-status REGISTERED
 2 {
 3    "domainInfos": [
 4        {
 5            "status": "REGISTERED",
 6            "name": "ExampleDomain"
 7        },
 8        {
 9            "status": "REGISTERED",
10            "name": "mytest"
11        }
12    ]
13 }
```

You can see deprecated domains by using `--registration-status DEPRECATED` with `list-domains`.

```
 1 $ aws swf list-domains --registration-status DEPRECATED
```

```
2  {
3      "domainInfos": [
4          {
5              "status": "DEPRECATED",
6              "name": "MyNeatNewDomain"
7          }
8      ]
9  }
```

You can also use `describe-domain` to get information about a deprecated domain.

```
1  $ aws swf describe-domain --name MyNeatNewDomain
2  {
3      "domainInfo": {
4          "status": "DEPRECATED",
5          "name": "MyNeatNewDomain"
6      },
7      "configuration": {
8          "workflowExecutionRetentionPeriodInDays": "0"
9      }
10 }
```

See Also

- deprecate-domain in the *AWS Command Line Interface Reference*
- describe-domain in the *AWS Command Line Interface Reference*
- list-domains in the *AWS Command Line Interface Reference*
- register-domain in the *AWS Command Line Interface Reference*

Troubleshooting AWS CLI Errors

After installing with `pip`, you may need to add the `aws` executable to your OS's `PATH` environment variable, or change its mode to make it executable.

Error: *aws: command not found*

You may need to add the `aws` executable to your OS's `PATH` environment variable.

- **Windows** –
- **macOS** –
- **Linux** –

If `aws` is in your `PATH` and you still see this error, it may not have the right file mode. Try running it directly.

```
1 $ ~/.local/bin/aws --version
```

Error: *permission denied*

Make sure that the `aws` script has a file mode that is executable. For example, **755**.

Run `chmod +x` to make the file executable.

```
1 $ chmod +x ~/.local/bin/aws
```

Error: *AWS was not able to validate the provided credentials*

The AWS CLI may be reading credentials from a different location than you expect. Run `aws configure list` to confirm that the correct credentials are used.

```
1 $ aws configure list
2      Name                    Value             Type    Location
3      ----                    -----             ----    --------
4   profile                <not set>             None    None
5 access_key     ****************XYVA shared-credentials-file
6 secret_key     ****************ZAGY shared-credentials-file
7    region                us-west-2     config-file    ~/.aws/config
```

If the correct credentials are in use, your clock may be out of sync. On Linux, macOS, or Unix, run `data` to check the time.

```
1 date
```

If your system clock is off, use `ntpd` to sync it.

```
1 sudo service ntpd stop
2 sudo ntpdate time.nist.gov
3 sudo service ntpd start
4 ntpstat
```

On Windows, use the date and time options in the control panel to configure your system clock.

Error: *An error occurred (UnauthorizedOperation) when calling the* CreateKeyPair *operation: You are not authorized to perform this operation.*

Your IAM user or role needs permission to call the API actions that correspond to the commands that you run with the AWS CLI. Most commands call a single action with a name that matches the command name; however, custom commands like `aws s3 sync` call multiple APIs. You can see which APIs a command calls by using the `--debug` option.